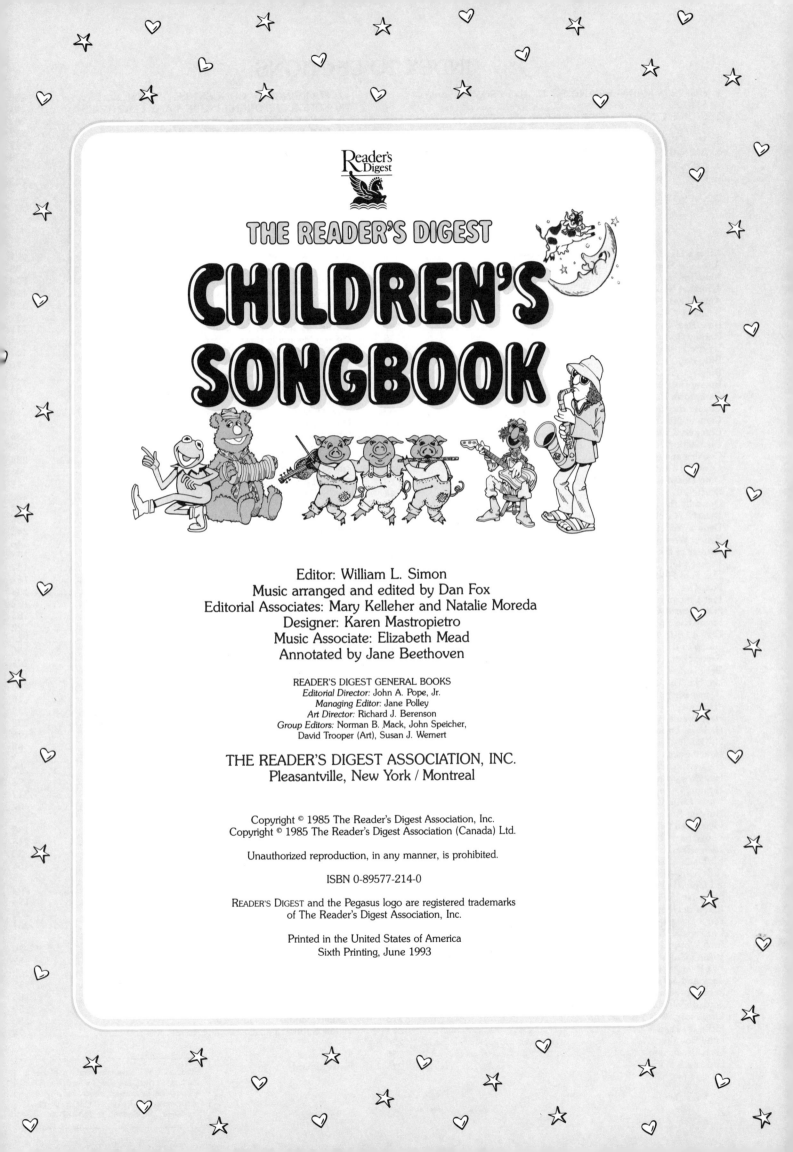

THE READER'S DIGEST
CHILDREN'S SONGBOOK

Editor: William L. Simon
Music arranged and edited by Dan Fox
Editorial Associates: Mary Kelleher and Natalie Moreda
Designer: Karen Mastropietro
Music Associate: Elizabeth Mead
Annotated by Jane Beethoven

READER'S DIGEST GENERAL BOOKS
Editorial Director: John A. Pope, Jr.
Managing Editor: Jane Polley
Art Director: Richard J. Berenson
Group Editors: Norman B. Mack, John Speicher,
David Trooper (Art), Susan J. Wernert

THE READER'S DIGEST ASSOCIATION, INC.
Pleasantville, New York / Montreal

ISBN 0-89577-214-0

Printed in the United States of America
Sixth Printing, June 1993

INDEX TO SECTIONS

INDEX TO SONGS

*Instrumental

Reader's Digest Fund for the Blind is publisher of the Large-Type Edition of *Reader's Digest.* For subscription information about this magazine, please contact Reader's Digest Fund for the Blind, Inc., Dept. 250, Pleasantville, N.Y. 10570.

INTRODUCTION

When you come right down to it, children today really aren't much different from the way their parents or grandparents were when *they* were children. Toys have changed (tin soldiers would probably refuse to fight in today's intergalactic star wars), computers replace textbooks, and six-year-olds use words that adults never heard before. But basically, kids are still kids . . . still sharing the special joys of childhood that we older folk remember from 20 or 30 or 50 or more years ago.

One of those special joys is music. And although bespangled rock-and-roll singers may be the children's idols of the moment, the nursery rhymes, nonsensical novelties and folk and holiday songs that delighted older generations also appeal to the newest generations — this year, next year and in the years to come.

In compiling the songs for this book, we reviewed personal and family favorites, old and new, looking for classics that adults and children — from toddlers to teenagers — could share. We read through and remembered *Mother Goose* and other nursery rhymes from long ago and far away. With guitar in hand, we sang old folk songs and folk songs that originated during the revival of the 1950s and '60s . . . from "Clementine" to "This Land Is Your Land" . . . all of them having the same honesty, simplicity and charm. We chuckled at the nonsense songs that were popular hits with adults in less "sophisticated" times, songs like "Barney Google" and "Mairzy Doats." Children, too, loved them then, and still will today. We selected songs from favorite movies, shows and cartoons, and some of the fine tunes from *Sesame Street* and The Muppets. And we skipped our way through party dances such as "The Alley Cat" and "The Bunny Hop." And then there were the teaching songs . . . and the rounds . . . and holiday songs like "Rudolph the Red-Nosed Reindeer" and everybody's once-a-year favorite, "Happy Birthday to You."

It was difficult choosing. But in the end, we brought together 131 songs that we older folk can share with young ones. Some of the songs may give us a chance to relive past delights; some, youngsters may be introducing to us for the first time.

After selecting the songs, we got to work to ensure that the *Children's Songbook* would be easy to use and enjoyable for the greatest number of people. We kept page-turning within a song to a minimum. In songs with many verses, where one may have some difficulty following from line to line, we used a Reader's Digest innovation — a tint through alternate verses, to keep the eye from wandering. We chose illustrations that would delight all and help young children recognize their favorite songs. And we told about each song — how and where the song was written (many, you'll find, just "growed"), what the people who wrote it were like, where it has been performed.

All in all, we've worked hard to make this the best songbook ever compiled for children, and we're happy with the result. We hope you and the young people in your life will share many happy hours with it.

A NOTE ON THE ARRANGEMENTS

All songs in the book have complete piano arrangements, except for the nursery rhymes in Sections 11 and 12 and the rounds in Section 13. These have been arranged in single-line format but with an optional harmony part in smaller notes.

In the 11 other sections, the melody of each song is repeated on a separate staff, making it more easily available to singers and young instrumentalists. Our arranger, Dan Fox, has also made the melodies easy for youngsters to sing, since he has usually kept them within the compass of a child's voice (middle C to E above). The melody can also be played on virtually any "C" instrument that reads in the treble clef, including the recorder. (If played alone, B-flat or E-flat instruments can play the melody line, but not in combination with each other or with any "C" instrument.)

The chord symbols (*i.e.,* C, G7, etc.) can be used for guitar, banjo, ukulele, mandolin or any other instrument that can play chords, including even very limited chord organs and autoharps. Chords can be simplified by omitting bass notes (C/E means a C chord with E in the bass — you would simply press the button for a C chord), or by omitting material in parentheses, as in G(7), or by using indicated alternate chords in parentheses, *i.e.,* D#dim (B7). If your instrument doesn't have the diminished chord, it probably *does* have a B7, which will be acceptable.

For guitarists who may not read music or who do not have a secure knowledge of chords, we have provided fretboard diagrams for all the basic chords used in the book. You will find these on pages 2 and 3 of the Lyric Booklet that accompanies this book.

The numbers below the melody notes are for people who play the "C" chord organ and/or melodica or any of the electronic keyboards that are so popular today. Eventually, of course, we hope that you or your favorite child musicians will want to learn to read the musical notes.

The Editors

THE MUPPET SHOW THEME

**Words and Music by
Jim Henson and Sam Pottle**

"It's time to get things started," sings Kermit the Frog . . . and *The Muppet Show* begins. During their five years on TV (not to mention reruns), Jim Henson's crew — Kermit, Miss Piggy, Fozzie Bear, Gonzo, the Swedish Chef, Animal, Rowlf, assorted chickens and others — entertained children *and* adults in more than 100 countries.

Bright rag tempo

mf

| C | Ebdim (D) | G(7) | C | Ebdim (D) |

It's time to play the mu - sic; It's time to
It's time to put on make - up; It's time to

| G(7) | C | C(7) | F | Fm |

light the lights;— It's time to meet the Mup - pets on *The*
dress up right;— It's time to raise the cur - tain on *The*

4

1.

Am (A♭+) G

3 3 3 3 5

Mup-pet Show_ to-night.

2.

D(7) G(7) C

3 3 3 2 1 8

Mup-pet Show_ to-night. To

F Bdim(G) C C(7) D(7) Bdim(G)

9 8 7 9 8 5 8 9 8 7 9

in - tro - duce Miss Pig - gy, That's what I'm here to

C C(7) F(7) E(7) A(⁷₄) A(7)

8 8 8 9 8 7 9 10 5 5

do. So it real - ly makes me hap - py To

E♭(7) D(7) G(7)

6 6 7 8 9

in - tro - duce_ to you *The indescribable, the incompatible, the unadorable...Miss Piggy!*

(More) ⟶

5

The Muppet Show Theme

Words and Music by Joe Raposo

The message of this song is simple: Have fun singing . . . and don't worry if it's not good enough for anyone else to hear. Many youngsters who watch *Sesame Street* come from Latin American countries where everyone speaks (and sings in) Spanish. Joe Raposo, who speaks Spanish himself, wrote the catchy tune for the program in that language, calling it "Canta," which, of course, means "Sing." Under its English title, "Sing!" was recorded by such stars as Bing Crosby, Barbra Streisand and Johnny Mathis, and The Carpenters' version was in the Top 40 for 11 weeks in 1973.

Moderately, with a lilt

Sing!

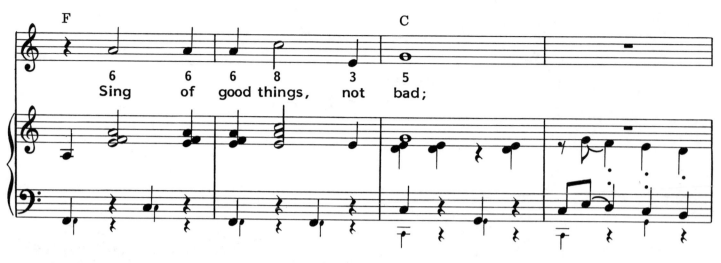

Sing of good things, not bad;

Sing of hap-py, not sad.

Sing!_____ Sing a song,_____ Make it

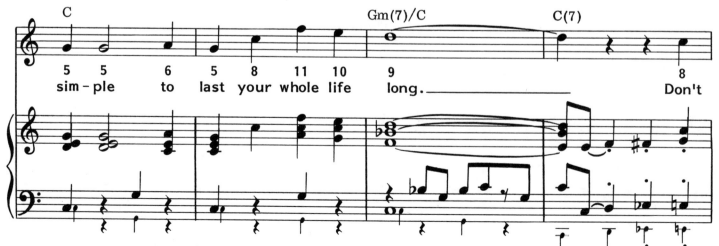

sim-ple to last your whole life long._____ Don't

worry that it's not good enough for anyone else to hear. Sing! Sing a song. La la do la da, La da la do la da, La da da la do la da.

Repeat and fade

9

GREEN
(Bein' Green)
Words and Music by Joe Raposo

Kermit the Frog likes himself just the way he is, green and beautiful. He sang this little "message" song by Joe Raposo in the earliest days of *Sesame Street*. "Bein' Green" makes you wonder what it would be like to be someone else. Would Kermit really want to be red or yellow or gold or some other brighter color? Certainly not! Even though it's sometimes not that easy, he's happy being green. And, like Kermit, aren't *you* glad you're *you*? Many singers have recorded Kermit's song, including Frank Sinatra, who made it a popular hit.

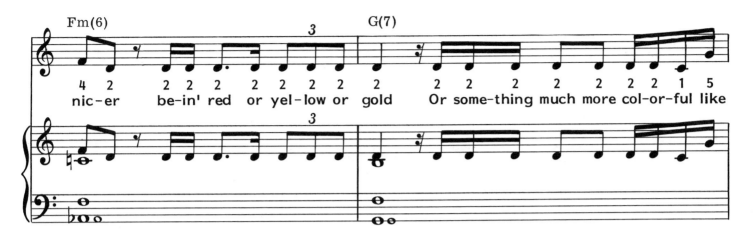

nic-er be-in' red or yel-low or gold Or some-thing much more col-or-ful like

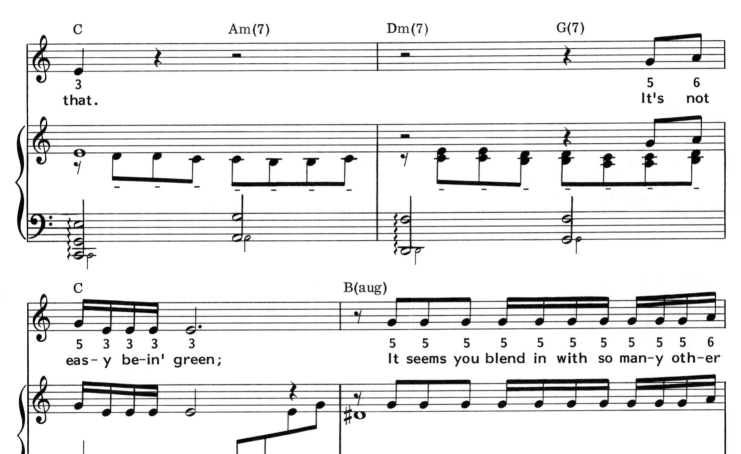

that. It's not

eas-y be-in' green; It seems you blend in with so man-y oth-er

or-di-nar-y things, And peo-ple tend to pass you

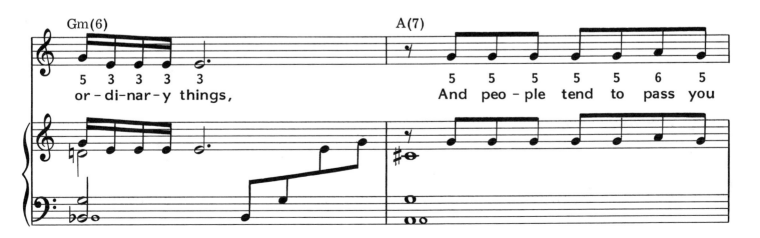

Green (Bein' Green)

port - tant like a moun-tain or tall like a tree.

When green is all there is to be, It could make you

won-der why, But why won-der, why won-der? I am green and it-'ll do fine; It's

beau-ti-ful__ and I think it's what I want to be.__

No One Like You

Words and Music by Andra Willis Muhoberac

In 1983, John Denver joined the Muppets in a TV special called *Rocky Mountain Holiday*. Many of the songs had themes that related to being outdoors. One of the exceptions was this lovely lullaby that Denver sang to Kermit's nephew, a small frog named Robin. There *is* no one exactly like Robin, or like any of the other Muppets, for that matter. And there's no one exactly like you!

I like your eyes;_____ I like your nose;_____ I like your mouth, Your ears, your hands, your toes. I like your face, It's real-ly

you; I like the things You say and do. There's not a sin - gle soul Who sees the skies The way you see them Through your eyes. And aren't you glad? You should be glad; There's no one, no one Ex-act-ly like you.

Rubber Duckie

When Ernie first sang "Rubber Duckie" on *Sesame Street*, he was sitting in the bathtub with his lovable toy, his "very best friend." Ernie's voice was that of Jim Henson, the master Muppeteer. The song is by Jeffrey Moss, one of the creators of the *Sesame Street* TV series and winner of Emmys both for

Words and Music by Jeffrey Moss

his writing and for his musical contributions to the show. "Rubber Duckie" has proven to be fun for young and old alike. In fact, this "children's song" went as high as No. 16 on the *pop* music charts in 1970. Even older people know that a favorite toy is a very special thing.

Rubber Duckie

I LOVE TRASH

Words and Music by Jeffrey Moss

A delightful tune and loving words make up Oscar the Grouch's ode to trash, written for him by Jeffrey Moss. From his home in a trash can on *Sesame Street*, Oscar sings of those things he loves . . . things "dirty or dingy or dusty . . . ragged or rotten or rusty," things that no one else likes but that are wonderful to him. It seems one Muppet's trash is another's treasure.

Lively waltz

Cm(7) F(7) Bb (Bbdim) Cm(7) F(7)

I love trash, An-y-thing dirt-y or din-gy or

Bb (Bbdim) Cm(7) F(7) Bb Bb(7)

dust-y, An-y-thing rag-ged or rot-ten or rust-y. _____ Oh,

I Love Trash

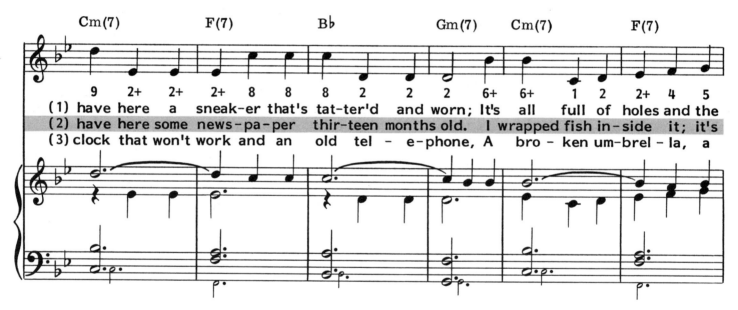

20

THE RAINBOW CONNECTION

from *The Muppet Movie*

**Words and Music by
Paul Williams and Kenny Ascher**

Kermit the Frog sings "The Rainbow Connection" at the opening of the Muppets' first major film. In *The Muppet Movie* (1979), which carried our favorite characters outside the TV studio to the real world for the first time, Miss Piggy, Fozzie Bear, Gonzo and other sidekicks join Kermit on the road to Hollywood in search of fame and fortune. During their travels they meet up with famous actors, actresses and comedians — Mel Brooks, Steve Martin, Madeleine Kahn and Orson Welles among them — and, yes, fans, they make it to Hollywood.

Moderately, with a lilt

1. Why are there so man-y songs a-bout rain-bows, And
2. Who said that ev-'ry wish would be heard and an-swered When
3. Have you been half a-sleep and have you heard voic - es? ___

(1) what's on the oth - er side?_____ Rain-bows are
(2) wished on the morn - ing star?_____ Some-bod-y
(3) I've heard them call-ing my name._____ Is this the

Last time to Coda ✛

23

Section 2
Songs from Some Favorite Movies and Shows

TOMORROW

Words by Martin Charnin

from Annie

Music by Charles Strouse

Little Orphan Annie, she of the red dress, curly red hair and pupil-less eyes, was brought to life in the 1977 Broadway musical *Annie*, which later became a movie.

"Tomorrow," the best-known song from the show, is the epitome of youthful optimism, with a "things-will-get-better" philosophy. So chin up. Tomorrow *will* be better.

The sun-'ll come out tomorrow, Bet your bot-tom dol-lar that to-
think-ing a-bout tomorrow Clears a-way the cob-webs and the

mor-row There'll be sun. Jus'
sor-row Till there's none.

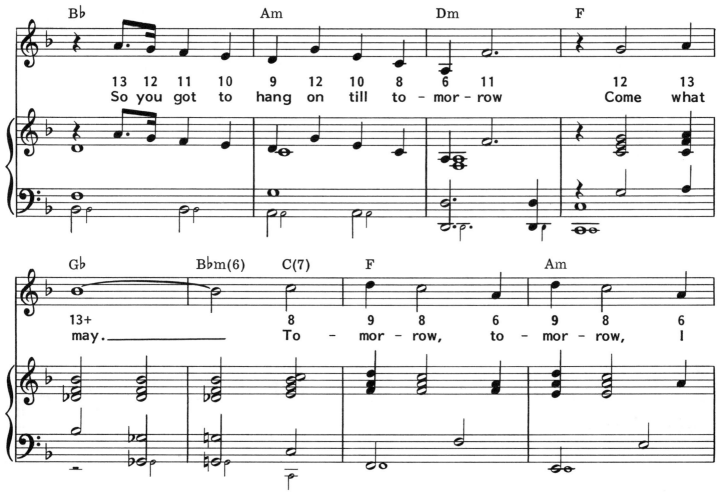

So you got to hang on till to-mor-row   Come what

may._____ To - mor - row, to - mor - row, I

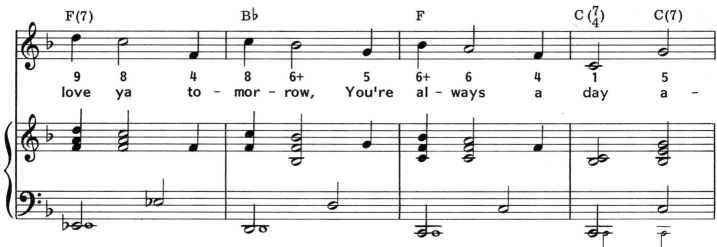

love ya to - mor - row, You're al - ways a day a -

way._____

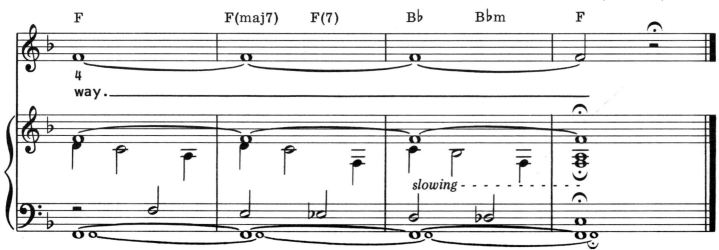

slowing - - - - - - - - - -

Ding-Dong! the Witch Is Dead

from *The Wizard of Oz*   **Words by E. Y. Harburg; Music by Harold Arlen**

This song is from the 1939 movie *The Wizard of Oz*, based on L. Frank Baum's book about the adventures of Dorothy (Judy Garland) in the land of Oz. There are two evil witches and a good witch in the story. The one in this song is the Wicked Witch of the East, who is killed when Dorothy's house, which was swept away by a tornado, lands on her! Later, Dorothy melts the Wicked Witch of the West. Dorothy is truly a heroine.

If I Only Had a Brain

(If I Only Had a Heart) (If I Only Had the Nerve)
from *The Wizard of Oz*
Words by E. Y. Harburg; Music by Harold Arlen

Ray Bolger was most convincing as the Scarecrow in *The Wizard of Oz*; his rubbery-legged dancing made him look jointless. He had a lot of fun even if he was supposedly without a brain. And he had more brain than he thought, just as the Tin Woodman had more heart and the Cowardly Lion more nerve than either of them suspected.

Allegretto (not fast, but with a lilt)

1. (Scarecrow) I could
2. (Tin Woodman) When a
3. (Cowardly Lion) Life is

(1) while a-way the hours__ con-fer-rin' with the flow'rs,__ con-
(2) man's an emp-ty ket-tle, he should be on his met-tle and
(3) sad, be-lieve me mis-sy, when you're born to be a sis-sy with-

(1) sult-in' with the rain,_____ And my head I'd be scratch-in' while my
(2) yet I'm torn a-part._____ Just be-cause I'm pre-sum-in' that I
(3) out the vim and verve,_____ But I could change my hab-its, nev-er-

(1) thoughts were bus-y hatch-in' If I on-ly had a brain._____ I'd un-
(2) could be kind-a hu-man If I on-ly had a heart._____ I'd be
(3) more be scared of rab-bits If I on-ly had the nerve._____ I'm a-

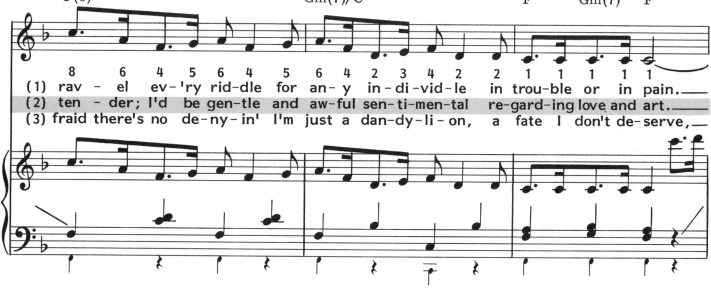

(1) rav-el ev-'ry rid-dle for an-y in-di-vid-le in trou-ble or in pain.__
(2) ten-der; I'd be gen-tle and aw-ful sen-ti-men-tal re-gard-ing love and art.__
(3) fraid there's no de-ny-in' I'm just a dan-dy-li-on, a fate I don't de-serve,__

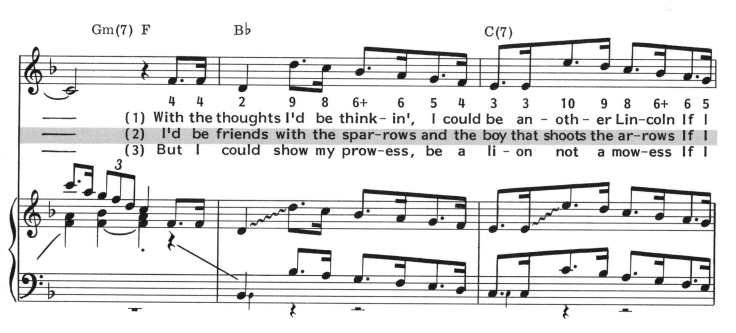

(1) With the thoughts I'd be think-in', I could be an-oth-er Lin-coln If I
(2) I'd be friends with the spar-rows and the boy that shoots the ar-rows If I
(3) But I could show my prow-ess, be a li-on not a mow-ess If I

If I Only Had a Brain

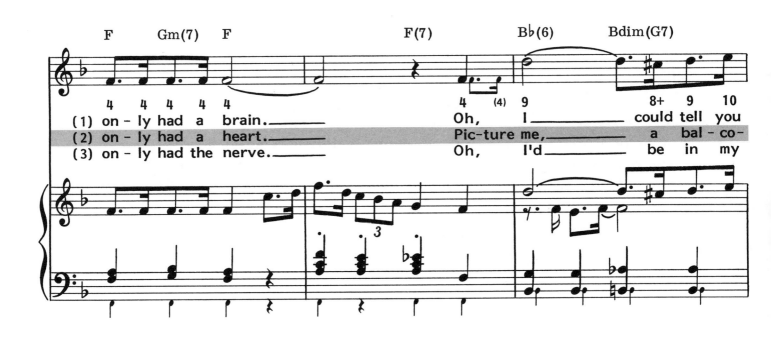

(1) on - ly had a brain._____   Oh, I _____ could tell you
(2) on - ly had a heart._____   Pic-ture me,_____ a bal-co-
(3) on - ly had the nerve._____   Oh, I'd _____ be in my

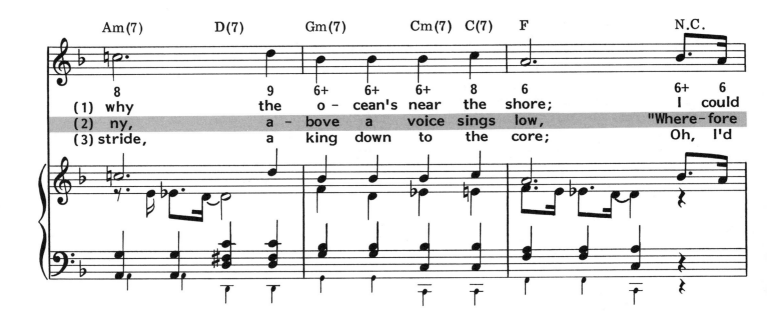

(1) why   the o - cean's near the shore;   I could
(2) ny,   a - bove a voice sings low,   "Where-fore
(3) stride,   a king down to the core;   Oh, I'd

(1) think of things I nev-er thunk be-fore.   And then I'd sit   And think some
(2) art thou, Ro - me - o?"   I hear a beat.
(3) roar the way I nev-er roared be-fore,   And then I'd rrrwoof   And roar some

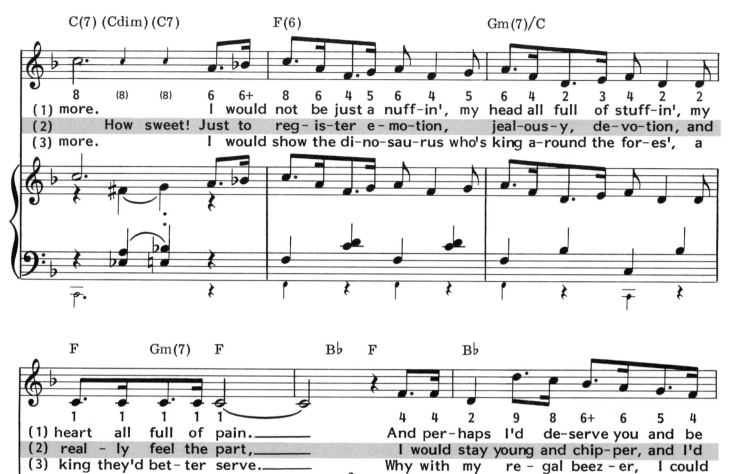

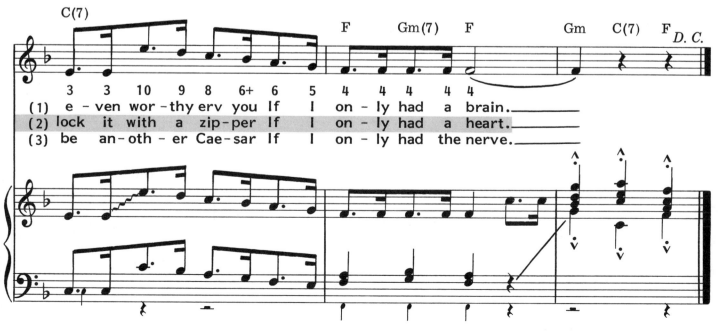

OVER THE RAINBOW

from *The Wizard of Oz*
Words by E. Y. Harburg
Music by Harold Arlen

Judy Garland was just a young starlet when she sang "Over the Rainbow" in *The Wizard of Oz*, but it became her theme song for the rest of her life. It was almost cut from the movie because some people thought it was too slow-paced and interfered with the action. Luckily, "Over the Rainbow" was kept in and won an Academy Award for Best Film Song of 1939. It's a song about dreaming and wishing and finding a trouble-free tomorrow. And remember, sometimes dreams do come true.

Chord symbols represent a simplified version of piano part.

Over the Rainbow

We're Off to See the Wizard

(The Wonderful Wizard of Oz)

from *The Wizard of Oz*   Words by E. Y. Harburg; Music by Harold Arlen

In *The Wizard of Oz*, Dorothy (Judy Garland) and her new-found friends —
Scarecrow (Ray Bolger), Cowardly Lion (Bert Lahr) and Tin Woodman
(Jack Haley) — dance and sing this song when they set off down the Yellow
Brick Road to seek the help of the wonderful wizard. Wouldn't it be nice
to have a *real* wizard to help you with your problems?

We're Off to See the Wizard

from *Hans Christian Andersen*
Words and Music by Frank Loesser

THE INCH WORM

Danny Kaye introduced "The Inch Worm" in the 1952 film *Hans Christian Andersen*, which had a sparkling score by Frank Loesser. There is something magical about a worm measuring a marigold, and the slow tempo of the song creates the feeling of the measuring process. Maybe that's what those worms really do. Who knows?

On the Good Ship Lollipop

from Bright Eyes

This song is associated with one of the most popular child stars of all time, Shirley Temple. The curly-haired moppet sang it in the 1934 movie *Bright Eyes*, when she was barely six years old. She grew up to become representative to the General Assembly of the United Nations (1969 – 70) and U.S. Ambassador to Ghana (1974 – 76).

Words and Music by Sidney Clare and Richard A. Whiting

sug-ar bowl do a toot-sie roll With the big bad dev-il's food cake. If you
eat too much, ooh! ooh! You'll a-wake with a tum-my ache. On the
good ship Lol-li-pop, It's a night trip, in-to bed you hop With
this com-mand:_____ "All a-board for Can-dy Land."

Do-Re-Mi

from *The Sound of Music*
Words by Oscar Hammerstein II
Music by Richard Rodgers

Maria Rainer, studying to be a nun in an Austrian abbey before World War II, seemed miscast in the stern religious setting. A wise Mother Abbess instead assigned her to serve temporarily as governess for the seven motherless children of Baron von Trapp. Maria, as the world now knows — thanks to Rodgers and Hammerstein's *The Sound of Music* — married the Baron and imbued the entire family with her love of life and of music. When the Nazis forced the Trapps to flee Austria, they came eventually to America, and for years, as The Trapp Family Singers, performed their songs for audiences, until the children married and settled down in many different places. In the show, Maria (first played on Broadway by Mary Martin and by Julie Andrews in the movie) uses "Do-Re-Mi" to teach the children the musical scale. It's easy to see why it has become one of the most popular "lessons" in musical history!

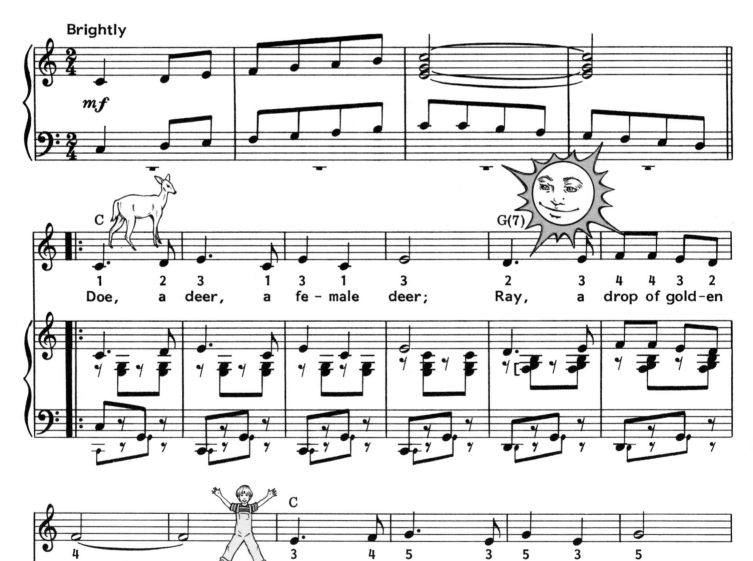

Doe, a deer, a fe – male deer; Ray, a drop of gold-en sun;_____ Me, a name I call my – self;

from *The Pink Panther*
Music by Henry Mancini

The Pink Panther

The Pink Panther (1963) was one of five movies in which Peter Sellers appeared as the bungling, ridiculously incompetent and hysterically funny Inspector Clouseau. As the film titles appeared, a cartooned pink panther moved across the screen, and this mysterious, jazzy theme was heard, played on a tenor saxophone and a trombone. There is really a great deal of fun in the mock-seriousness of Henry Mancini's award-winning music, considering the movie that was to follow.

Tempo mysterioso

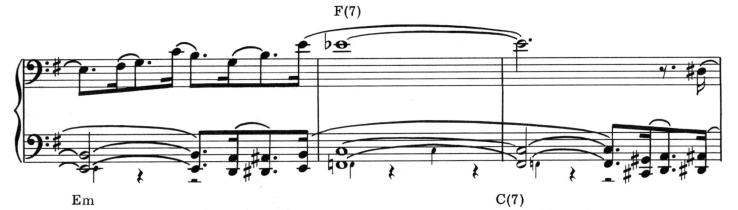

I Whistle a Happy Tune

from *The King and I*

Words by Oscar Hammerstein II; Music by Richard Rodgers

The English actress Gertrude Lawrence introduced "I Whistle a Happy Tune" in *The King and I* (1951), one of the many award-winning Broadway musicals (it also was made into a movie) by Richard Rodgers and Oscar Hammerstein. It was the show's opening number, sung by the character Anna Leonowens to her son as they arrived in Bangkok, where Anna would become teacher to the princes and princesses of the royal court. As Anna faced her uncertain future, she and her son both needed some encouragement. *You'll* be whistling this catchy tune whether or not you feel afraid.

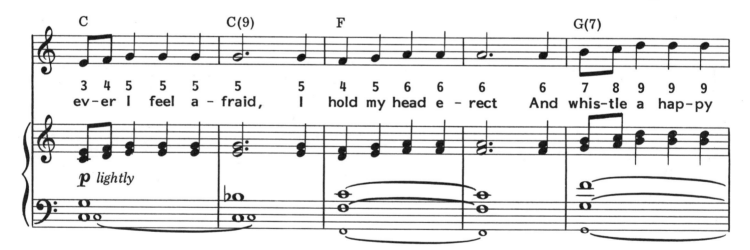

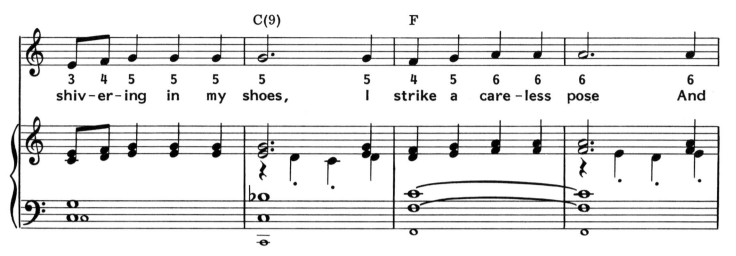

shiv-er-ing in my shoes, I strike a care-less pose And

whis-tle a hap-py tune, And no one ev-er knows I'm a-

fraid.___ The re-sult of this de-cep-tion is

ver-y strange to___ tell, For when I fool the peo-ple I fear, I

I Whistle a Happy Tune

Who's Afraid of the Big Bad Wolf?

from *The Three Little Pigs*

Words and Music by Frank E. Churchill

Additional words by Ann Ronell

Walt Disney's *The Three Little Pigs* (1933) produced this surprising hit song. Actually, all of the little pigs *should* have been afraid, but only the third piglet was wary and wise enough to build his house of strong bricks and so keep big bad wolfie away from his door.

Who's a‑fraid of the big bad wolf, big bad wolf, big bad wolf?

Who's a‑fraid of the big bad wolf? Tra la la la la.

52

Who's Afraid of the Big Bad Wolf?

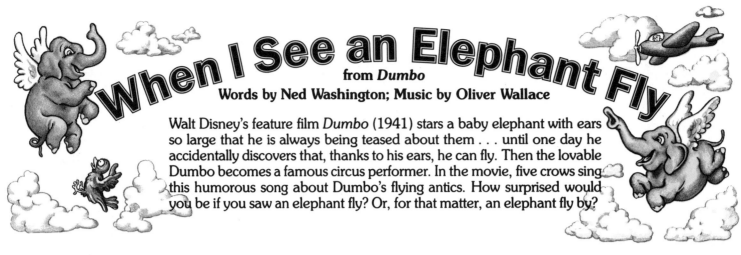

When I See an Elephant Fly

from *Dumbo*

Words by Ned Washington; Music by Oliver Wallace

Walt Disney's feature film *Dumbo* (1941) stars a baby elephant with ears so large that he is always being teased about them . . . until one day he accidentally discovers that, thanks to his ears, he can fly. Then the lovable Dumbo becomes a famous circus performer. In the movie, five crows sing this humorous song about Dumbo's flying antics. How surprised would you be if you saw an elephant fly? Or, for that matter, an elephant fly by?

Moderately, with a swing

When I See an Elephant Fly

In 1937, Walt Disney released *Snow White and the Seven Dwarfs,* his first feature-length animated film. It had taken a staff of 750 people more than three years to create the million drawings that went into the making of the movie. Disney based it on the Grimm brothers' fairy tale "Snow-drop." As the familiar story unfolds, Snow

WITH A SMILE AND A SONG

from *Snow White and the Seven Dwarfs*
Words by Larry Morey; Music by Frank Churchill

White's jealous stepmother orders a huntsman to kill her and sends her off to the forest with him. But the huntsman lets Snow White go, and she wanders alone in the frightening woods. When she discovers the friendly birds and animals looking at her wide-eyed, she laughs and sings this lighthearted formula for happiness.

Moderately

With a smile and a song,_____ Life is just like a

bright, sun-ny day. Your cares fade a-way,_____ And your heart is

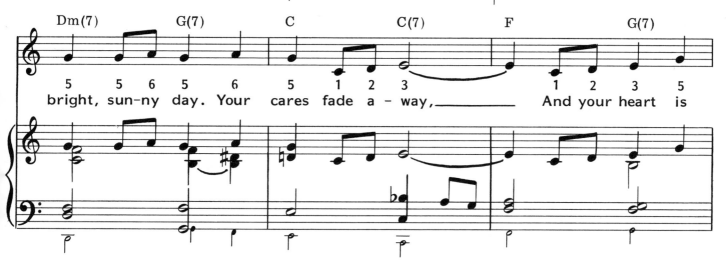

With a Smile and a Song

Whistle While You Work

from *Snow White and the Seven Dwarfs*
Words by Larry Morey; Music by Frank Churchill

In one scene in *Snow White*, friendly birds and animals lead Snow White to a little cottage in the forest. It is so dirty and in such a state of disarray that Snow White starts tidying it up. Her new woodland friends help as she sings this cheerful song. The birds whistle along with her. Wouldn't it be nice to have helpers like these when you have to clean your room?

One Song

from *Snow White and the Seven Dwarfs*
Words by Larry Morey
Music by Frank Churchill

In the final part of *Snow White,* the Prince finds the sleeping Snow White and pours out his heart to her as he sings "One Song." He has one song, one heart, one love . . . only for her. The beauty of the music alone should have been capable of breaking the magic spell Snow White was under, but it wasn't until the Prince kissed her that she opened her eyes.

"HEIGH-HO"

(The Dwarfs' Marching Song)

from *Snow White and the Seven Dwarfs*

Words by Larry Morey; Music by Frank Churchill

In *Snow White and the Seven Dwarfs*, Walt Disney gave each of the dwarfs a name and special personality traits that went with it — something the dwarfs didn't possess in the Grimms' original fairy tale. The impish septet — Doc, Happy, Dopey, Grumpy, Sleepy, Sneezy and Bashful — manage to work, walk and do just about everything in time with the music they sing in the movie. "Heigh-Ho" introduces our little friends as they head home to their cottage after working in the mine. What a surprise is waiting for them there!

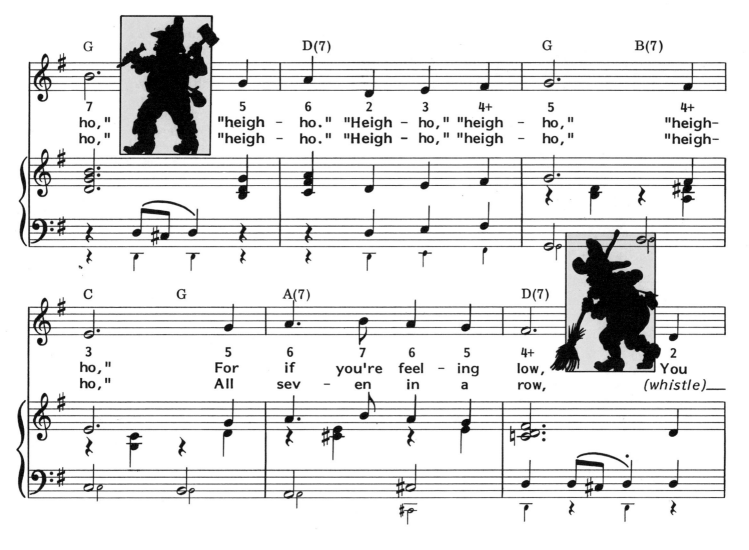

G   D(7)   G   B(7)

7   5   6   2   3   4+   5   4+

ho,"   "heigh - ho." "Heigh - ho," "heigh - ho,"   "heigh-
ho,"   "heigh - ho." "Heigh - ho," "heigh - ho,"   "heigh-

C   G   A(7)   D(7)

3   5   6   7   6   5   4+   2

ho,"   For   if   you're feel - ing   low,   You
ho,"   All   sev - en   in   a   row,   *(whistle)*

C   G   C   Cm

3   5   2   2   3   4+   5   8   8

pos - i - tive - ly   can't   go   wrong   With   a
                                 With   a

G   D(7) | G   D(7) | 2. G

1.

7   6   5   2   3   4+   5

"heigh,"   "heigh - ho." "Heigh - ho," "heigh -
"heigh,"   "heigh -   ho."

67

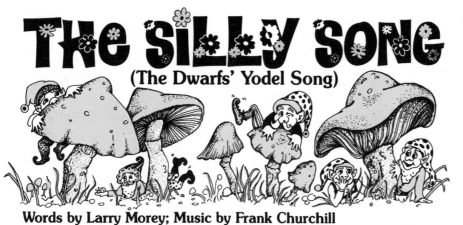

The Silly Song
(The Dwarfs' Yodel Song)

Words by Larry Morey; Music by Frank Churchill

from *Snow White and the Seven Dwarfs*

For *Snow White*, Walt Disney was presented with one large Oscar and seven small ones, one for each of the dwarfs. This is one of the tunes the charming little elves sing (and dance to) in the movie. Between verses, they yodel. (That's why it is also called "The Dwarfs' Yodel Song.") Outside, the birds and animals press beaks and noses against the cottage windows to get a better look. You might have, too . . . to see a spectacle such as this.

Lively, in 2 (♩=1 beat)

1. I'd
2. The
3. I
4. We

(1) like to dance and tap my feet, But they won't keep in rhy-thm. You
(2) min-ute af-ter I was born, I did-n't have a night-ie. So
(3) chased a pole-cat up a tree, Way out up-on a limb,___ An'
(4) used to have a bill-y goat; We had him dis-in-fect-ed. He

(1) see, I washed them both to-day, And I can't do noth-in' with 'em.
(2) I tied my whis-kers round my legs And used them for a did-ie.
(3) when he got the best o' me, I___ got the worst o' him.___
(4) could have slept in Grump-y's bed, But the bill-y goat ob-ject-ed.

68

Hi-Diddle-Dee-Dee
(An Actor's Life for Me)

Pinocchio (1940) was Walt Disney's second full-length cartoon feature and his first to win an Oscar for its musical score. Based on a familiar children's tale, *Pinocchio* tells the story of a wooden puppet who grapples with the lure of evil pleasure as he tries to be good so that he can become a real boy. A fox named J. Worthington Foulfellow sings "Hi-Diddle-Dee-Dee" as he tries to persuade Pinocchio to join a marionette troupe. His lively song is most convincing.

from *Pinocchio*
Words by Ned Washington
Music by Leigh Harline

Hi - did-dle-dee - dee, An ac - tor's life for me:

high silk hat and a sil - ver cane, A watch of gold with a dia-mond chain.

Give a Little Whistle

from *Pinocchio*
Words by Ned Washington; Music by Leigh Harline

In the original Italian story of *Pinocchio,* the cricket played only a brief role. But in Disney's movie, Jiminy Cricket is an important character; he acts as Pinocchio's conscience. Without a friendly cricket at your side, just take Jiminy's advice and "always let your conscience be your guide."

Moderately fast

When you get in trou-ble And you don't know right from wrong, Give a lit-tle
When you meet temp-ta-tion And the urge is ver-y strong,

whis-tle *(whistle),* Give a lit-tle whis-tle *(whistle).*

Not just a lit-tle squeak, Puck-er up and blow.

Yellow Submarine

from *Yellow Submarine*
Words and Music by
John Lennon and Paul McCartney

This is the theme song of The Beatles' *Yellow Submarine* (1968), a pop-art animated film with wonderful colors. In the movie, the Blue Meanies, who make happiness impossible, invade peaceful Pepperland, home of Sgt. Pepper's Lonely Hearts Club Band. Eventually, good triumphs over evil. Fred, conductor of the band, and John, Paul, George and Ringo (who all live in the yellow submarine) drive the Blue Meanies away.

(Optional kazoo solo—————————)

Yellow Submarine

Popeye is one of the most popular cartoon characters of all time. He has been fighting Bluto (originally called Brutus), courting the fickle Olive Oyl, putting up with hamburger-loving Wimpy and rescuing Olive's nephew Swee' Pea from danger for over 50 years. But Popeye is best known for the strength he gets from eating spinach. Generations of children who don't like that vegetable have been told to eat it if they wanted to be "big and strong like Popeye." The

squinty-eyed, pipe-smoking sailor started in the comic pages in newspapers and later was transformed into a cartoon for the movies. He finally flexed his famous tattooed muscles on television in hundreds of *Popeye* episodes, all of which ended roughly the same way — good triumphed over evil and/ or Bluto received his just reward. Is there a child anywhere in the world who does not know of the adventures of the famous Popeye the Sailor Man?

I'M POPEYE THE SAILOR MAN

Words and Music by Sammy Lerner

I'm Popeye the Sailor Man

79

CASPER THE FRIENDLY GHOST

Words by Mack David; Music by Jerry Livingston

Here's the theme song of a cartoon series of the same name that delighted children for years. Casper, the ghostly little star, was always looking for someone to play with, but older people shrieked and ran away when they saw him. Some children, however, understood Casper and his friendly ways and played with him. Do you think you'd have a good time with Casper — "the friendliest ghost you've seen" — if he visited you?

Cas - per the friend-ly ghost, The friend-li-est ghost you know. Though
Cas - per the friend-ly ghost, He could-n't be bad or mean. He'll

grown-ups might look at him with fright, The chil-dren all love him so.
romp and play, sing and dance all day, The

friend-li-est ghost you've seen. He al - ways says "Hel -

80

(How Much Is) That Doggie in the Window

Patti Page had a million-seller with her 1953 recording of this amusing novelty song, complete with the sound of a barking dog. In addition, through multitrack taping, the disc featured two Pattis singing together and thus made Miss Page a pioneer in modern recording techniques. The song was first introduced on a children's album, and its popular appeal was instantly spotted by disc jockeys. It was then released as a single record and stayed on the best-selling charts for eight weeks. A small dog in a shop window is a hard thing for anyone to resist . . . especially if it has a waggly tail.

Words and Music by Bob Merrill

Moderate waltz

mf

C   (C#°)   G(7)   *Bark*   *Bark*

How much is that dog - gie in the win - dow, _____ The one with the

sim.

C   (C#°)   G(7)   C   (C#°)

wag - gle - y tail? _____ How much is that dog - gie in the

win-dow?_____ I do hope that dog-gie's for sale._____

I must take a trip to Cal - i - for - nia _____ And leave my poor
I read in the pa - pers there are rob - bers_____ With flash-lights that

sweet-heart a - lone._____ If he has a dog, he won't be
shine in the dark._____ My love needs a dog - gie to pro-

lone - some,_____ And the dog - gie will have a good home._____
tect him_____ And scare them a - way with one bark._____

Melody

My Dog's Bigger Than Your Dog

Words and Music by Tom Paxton

Composer and folksinger Tom Paxton surely is observant. Who has not bragged about something he or she has that is better than anyone else's . . . even if it isn't? We all need to feel important sometimes, and then a little exaggeration goes a long way in making us feel good. The child in this song brags about his dog, his dad, his family's car and his mom . . . but do you think that his mom might object to the way he boasts about her?

Brightly

My dog's big-ger than your dog;   My dog's big-ger than yours.
Our car's fast-er than your car;   Our car's fast-er than yours.

My dog's big-ger and he chas-es mail-men. My dog's big-ger than yours.
It has a loud horn; it bumps the oth-er cars. Our car's fast-er than yours.

84

My dad's tough-er than your dad; My dad's tough-er than yours.
My mom's old-er than your mom; My mom's old-er than yours.

My dad's tough-er and he yells loud-er and My dad's tough-er than yours.
She takes smell-y baths; she hides the gray hairs. My mom's old-er than yours.

Chorus

I'm not a-fraid of the dark an-y-more; I can tie my shoes. I have been to the

coun-try, And I am go-ing to school. Nyaa nyaa na na na Nyaa.

85

OH WHERE, OH WHERE HAS MY LITTLE DOG GONE?

This German folk tune was first published in Leipzig in 1847. There was no dog in the song then — it was called "Zu Lauterbach Hab' Ich Mein Strumpf Verloren" (At Lauterbach I Lost My Sock). In 1864, American composer Septimus Winner, who also wrote some Civil War songs and created the lyrics for another old-fashioned favorite, "Listen to the Mocking Bird," borrowed the tune, wrote English words for it and called the result "Der Deitcher's Dog." A dog that is hiding can be hard to find. But sometimes big eyes and a wagging tail will give it away.

Moderately, in 1 (♩. = 1 beat)

Oh where, oh where has my lit-tle dog gone? Oh where, oh where can he be?_____ With his ears cut short and his tail cut long, Oh where, oh where can he be?_____

The Animal Fair

This children's favorite is a 19th-century minstrel song. Minstrel shows were the first uniquely American form of entertainment and laid the foundations for the development of our American musical theater. They featured white performers made up in blackface, and their material drew heavily from Negro culture. Minstrel shows, featuring such groups as The Christy Minstrels, were popular from 1850 to 1870, but the advent of vaudeville, followed by movies and radio, brought an end to this form of entertainment. Minstrel songs were frequently nonsensical and full of fantasy. Many tell of animals in preposterous situations, as this song does. The monk's fate was probably sad.

Gaily

I went to the an-i-mal fair;___ The birds and the beasts were there.___ The big ba-boon by the light of the moon Was comb-ing his au-burn hair.___ You what be-came of the monk?

ought to have seen_ the monk;___ He jumped on the el-e-phant's trunk.___ The el-e-phant sneezed_ and fell on his knees, And

THE FOX

"The Fox," an American folk song, dates back to the time when the United States was a group of 13 British colonies — before independence from England and before George Washington became the first president. In old nursery rhymes, the lady that is here called Mother Flipper-Flopper is also known as "Widdle-Waddle," "Hipple-Hopple," "Chittle-Chattle" and "Slipper-Slopper." But whatever her name, she was not fast enough in alerting John, and the fox ran off, taking the tasty gray goose back to his family for their dinner. That fox really had a fine time in the town-o.

With spirit

(1) fox went out in the chil - ly night; He prayed for the moon to
(2) ran till he came to a great big bin; The ducks and the geese were
(3) grabbed a gray goose by the neck and threw A duck a-cross his back.

(1) give him light. He'd man - y a mile to go that night Be-fore he reached the
(2) kept there - in. A cou - ple of you will grease my chin Be-fore I leave this
(3) He didn't mind their quack quack quack And their legs all dang - ling

4. (Then old) Mother Flipper-Flopper jumped out of bed,
   And out of the window she stuck her head;
   Said, "Get up, John, the gray goose is gone,
   And the fox is in the town-o, town-o, town-o"; *etc.*

5. So John, he ran to the top of the hill,
   And he blew his horn both loud and shrill.
   The fox he said, "I better flee with my kill,
   Or they'll soon be on my trail-o, trail-o, trail-o"; *etc.*

6. He ran till he came to his cozy den
   And there were his little ones, eight, nine and ten.
   They said, "Daddy, you better go back again,
   'Cause it must be a mighty fine town-o, town-o, town-o"; *etc.*

7. So the fox and his wife without any strife,
   They cut up the goose with a fork and a knife.
   They never had such a supper in their lives,
   And the little ones chewed on the bones-o, bones-o, bones-o"; *etc.*

Tom Paxton, who wrote this song, spent many of his formative years in Oklahoma, the state in which the legendary folksinger-songwriter Woody Guthrie was born. Paxton admits he is indebted to Guthrie, as are many other

folk-song writers. Who doesn't like going to the zoo? This song captures all the excitement of a visit to the zoo as well as the antics of the animals. One day at the zoo hardly seems enough . . . that's why "Momma's taking us to the zoo tomorrow."

Going to the Zoo

Words and Music by Tom Paxton

1. Dad-dy's tak-ing us to the zoo to-mor-row,— Zoo to-mor-row,—
2. See the el-e-phant with the long trunk swing-in',—Great big— ears and
3. See— all the mon-keys scritch scritch scratch-in',—Jump-in' all a-round and

(1) zoo to-mor-row.— Dad-dy's tak-ing us to the
(2) long trunk swing-in',— Sniff-in' up— pea-nuts with the
(3) scritch scritch scratch-in',— Hang-in' by their long tails—

(1) zoo to-mor-row;— We can— stay all day. We're go-ing to the
(2) long trunk swing-in'.—
(3) scritch scritch scratch-in'.—

4. Big black bear all huff huff a-puffin';
   Coat's too heavy, he's huff huff a-puffin'.
   Don't get too near the huff huff a-puffin',
   Or you won't stay all day.
   Chorus

5. Seals in the pool all honk honk honkin',
   Catchin' fish and honk honk honkin',
   Little seals honk honk honkin' *(high-pitched voice)*.
   We can stay all day.
   Chorus

6. *(slower tempo)* We stayed all day and we're gettin' sleepy,
   Sittin' in the car gettin' sleep sleep sleepy.
   Home already and we're sleep sleep sleepy.
   We have stayed all day.

   We've been to the zoo, zoo, zoo.
   So have you, you, you.
   You came too, too, too.
   We've been to the zoo, zoo, zoo.

7. *(original tempo)* Momma's taking us to the zoo tomorrow,
   Zoo tomorrow, zoo tomorrow.
   Momma's taking us to the zoo tomorrow;
   We can stay all day.
   Chorus

Words by
Walt Barrows

Music by
Bernard Zaritzky

The Little White Duck

All of the pond creatures in "The Little White Duck" are so glad to be sitting in the water. What a shame the song has such a sad ending, with no one left but the little red snake. Film star Danny Kaye made a recording of "The Little White Duck" in the 1950s, and so did many folksingers, including Burl Ives.

4. (There's a) little red snake (sss)
Lying in the water,
A little red snake (sss)
Doing what he oughter.
He frightened the duck and the frog so bad;
He ate the little bug and he said,
"I'm glad I'm a little red snake
Lying in the water."
Sss, sss, sss.

5. Now there's nobody left (sob)
Sitting in the water,
Nobody left (sob)
Doing what he oughter.
There's nothing left but the lily pad;
The duck and the frog ran away.
It's sad that there's nobody left
Sitting in the water.
Boo, hoo, hoo.

Me and My Teddy Bear

Words by Jack Winters; Music by J. Fred Coots

A 1953 album of children's songs by Rosemary Clooney included this one about a boy
and his teddy bear . . . a slightly worn-out bear that was loved just the same. Do you have a
special toy or doll that you particularly love? J. Fred Coots, who composed this tune,
wrote more than 3,000 songs, including "Santa Claus Is Comin' to Town" (see page 238).

95

OLD MacDONALD HAD A FARM

Old MacDonald's farm certainly was a noisy place, what with all those animals mooing, oinking, quacking and neighing. Each time you add an animal, you should work backward through the animal sounds. For example, after singing "Here a quack, there a quack, ev'rywhere a quack-quack," go back and sing "With an oink-oink here and an oink-oink there, / Here an oink, there an oink, ev'rywhere an oink-oink," followed by "With a moo-moo here and a moo-moo there, / Here a moo, there a moo, ev'rywhere a moo-moo," finally ending with "Old MacDonald had a farm, / E-I-E-I-O." It's possible to sing this old favorite all night long if you can think of enough animals.

1. Old Mac-Don-ald had a farm, E-I-E-I O,_____ And
2. Old Mac-Don-ald had a farm, E-I-E-I O,_____ And
3. Old Mac-Don-ald had a farm, E-I-E-I O,_____ And

(1) on his farm he had a cow, E-I-E-I-O._____ With a
(2) on his farm he had a pig, E-I-E-I-O._____ With an
(3) on his farm he had a duck, E-I-E-I-O._____ With a

96

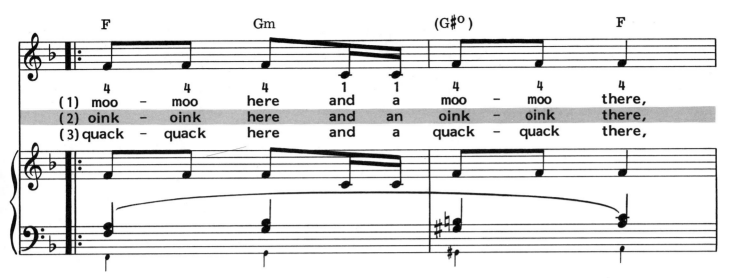

4. Old MacDonald had a farm,
E-I-E-I-O,
And on his farm he had a horse,
E-I-E-I-O.
With a neigh-neigh here and a neigh-neigh there, *etc.*

5. Old MacDonald had a farm,
E-I-E-I-O,
And on his farm he had a donkey,
E-I-E-I-O.
With a hee-haw here, *etc.*

6. Old MacDonald had a farm,
E-I-E-I-O,
And on his farm he had some chickens,
E-I-E-I-O.
With a chick-chick here, *etc.*

For additional verses, add your own animals.

97

THE TEDDY BEARS' PICNIC

Words by Jimmy Kennedy

Did you ever wonder what your toys do when you are not home? The soldiers probably march around the house. The dolls dress up and invite friends to a tea party. And your teddy bear may go down to the woods for a picnic. Composer John Bratton must have wondered about toys, too. He wrote the jaunty melody of this song as a piano piece in 1907. Jimmy Kennedy added the words 40 years later.

Music by John W. Bratton

Slow march tempo

If you go down in the woods to-day, You're sure of a big sur-prise.___ If you go down in the woods to-day, You'd bet-ter go in dis-guise,___ For ev - 'ry bear that ev-er there was Will gath-er there for cer-tain be-cause To-

I LOVE LITTLE PUSSY

"I Love Little Pussy" is an old Mother Goose rhyme, which means that children have delighted in singing this song for at least several hundred years. Kittens don't seem to have changed much over the centuries. Children and pussycats are still natural companions.

Gently, in 1 (♩. = 1 beat)

I love lit-tle pus-sy, Her coat is so warm, And
if I don't hurt her, She'll do me no harm.
I'll sit by the fire And
I'll not pull her tail Nor
give her some food, And pus-sy will love me Be-cause I am good.
drive her a-way. Lit-tle pus-sy and I Ver-y gent-ly will play.

101

The Whistler

There are no words to this song, but there are plenty of sound effects. You may not be able to hear much of the whistler with all that howling and woofing going on. Try making the sound effects. They're lots of fun. But what's that meow doing at the end of this piece? Arthur Pryor, who wrote this tune, was the solo trombone player in John Philip Sousa's band back in the early 1900s. He eventually became a well-known band director himself. If you ever decide to study the trombone, you'll soon become familiar with more of his compositions.

and His Dog

Music by Arthur Pryor
Adapted and arranged by Dan Fox

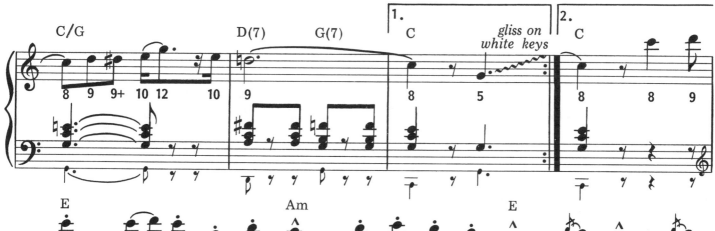

(pant rapidly)

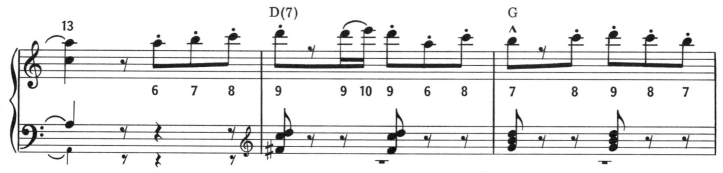

The Whistler and His Dog

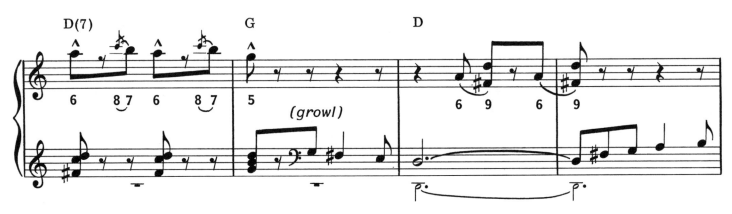

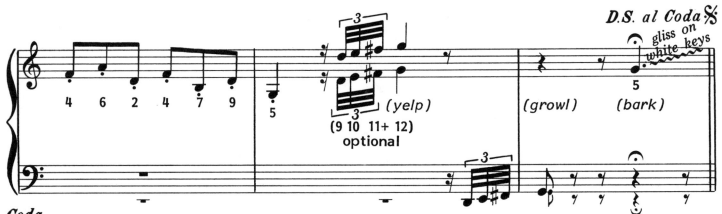

WILLIE THE WHISTLING GIRAFFE

Words by Rube Goldberg; Music by Ruth Cleary Patterson

Rube Goldberg, who won a Pulitzer Prize in 1948 for his convoluted cartoon contraptions in *The New York Sun*, wrote this song in 1951. Ruth Cleary Patterson supplied the tune. Despite the lyric's claim that giraffes have "no vocal cords," the long-necked animals can make sounds (although they seldom do). Maybe giraffes just don't have too much to say . . . unless, that is, they swallow a whistle.

The tall gi-raffe whose neck is long Can see for miles a-round, But the poor thing has no vo-cal cords, So he can-not make a sound.

Willie the Whistling Giraffe

hide in the this-tle and whis-tle and whis-tle, The an-i-mals all would o-bey. Now he's Wil-lie, the whis-tling gi-raffe; We can all hear him whis-tle and laugh. All the an-i-mals too Call him King of the Zoo, King Wil-lie, the whis-tling gi-raffe.

Pussy-cat, Pussy-cat

The queen mentioned in this nursery tune is reported to be the great English queen, Elizabeth I, who lived in the late 1500s. The song supposedly describes an incident that actually took place. But then, cats have been chasing mice under chairs for years and years, probably frightening the occupants of the chairs at least as much as the mice.

Brightly, in 1 (each ♩.=1 beat)

Pus - sy - cat, pus - sy - cat, Where have you been? "I've been to Lon - don to vis - it the Queen." Pus - sy - cat, pus - sy - cat, What did you there? "I fright-ened a lit - tle mouse un-der her chair."

speed up

Absolute Nonsense

I'm a Little Teapot

Written by Clarence Kelley and George Sanders

This song is usually acted out by putting one hand on your hip to be the handle and the other on your shoulder to be the spout. Then, do the motions in reverse. But don't lean over too far when "pouring out," or you and your tea may wind up on the floor.

I'm a lit–tle tea–pot, short and stout. Here is my han–dle;
I'm a ver–y spe–cial pot, it's true; Here let me show you

here is my spout. When I get all steamed up,
what it can do. I can change my han – dle

then I shout, "Tip me o–ver and pour me out."
and my spout; Tip me o–ver and pour me out.

A-Tisket A-Tasket

Words and Music by Ella Fitzgerald and Van Alexander

Ella Fitzgerald, the great jazz singer, scored one of the biggest hits of the Swing Era with her 1938 recording of "A-Tisket A-Tasket" — an American nursery rhyme that dates back to 1879. During the 11 weeks that the song was on *The Hit Parade*, it held the No. 1 position for six of them. This familiar children's game song has had some fancy jazzing up in this version by Miss Fitzgerald and Van Alexander. But the music remains deceivingly cheerful considering the fact that it's not much fun to lose something you love.

Chickery Chick

Words by Sylvia Dee; Music by Sidney Lippman

"Chickery Chick" provided bandleader Sammy Kaye of Swing and Sway fame with a best-selling recording in 1945. Composers Sylvia Dee and Sidney Lippman based the song on another tune, which began, "In China once there was a man / Whose name was Chickery Chickery Chan." Despite its seeming nonsense, "Chickery Chick" offers some good advice: When things get boring, try something new. This creative chick certainly said a mouthful of silly words. Can you sing them?

Chickery Chick

Words and Music by
Lee Ricks and Slim Gaillard

Slim Gaillard had the magic formula for successful novelty songs. In 1948 he had a hit with this song, which he adapted from an old tune for children. He also

wrote "Cement Mixer" and "The Flat Foot Floogee" (see pages 121 and 140). "Down by the Station" extols all of the excitement of riding on a train. The days of the "puffer bellies" are gone and forgotten, but train riding is still an awful lot of fun.

Moderately, in 2 (♩ = 1 beat)

This is for the peo-ple who nev-er rode the train,

Wheth-er in Cal - i - for - nia or e - ven up in Maine.

Makes no dif-f'rence if you're two or a hun-dred and two,

116

You'll get a treat when you or-der a seat on the ole choo - choo.

Chorus

Down by the sta - tion ear - ly in the morn - ing, See the lit - tle puff - er bel - lies all in a row. See the sta - tion-mas - ter turn the lit - tle han - dle, Chug, chug, toot, toot, Off we go.

The Marvelous Toy

Words and Music by Tom Paxton

This is another children's song by Tom Paxton, a real American troubadour. "The Marvelous Toy" was one of the first songs that Paxton submitted for publication. The words describe a rather unusual toy, complete with the sounds it made. After singing this song, try drawing a picture of "The Marvelous Toy." What do *you* think it is?

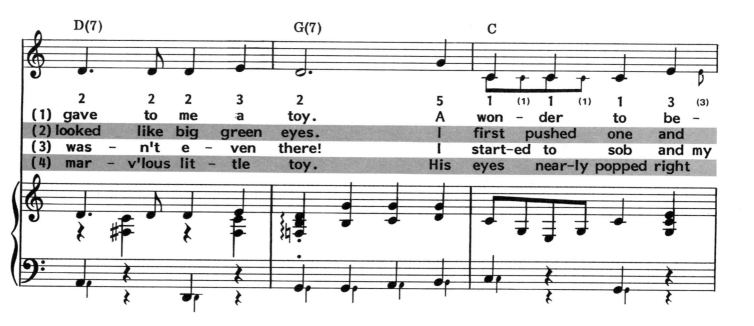

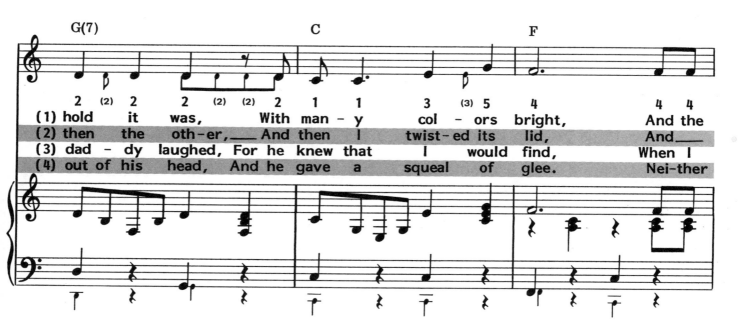

The Marvelous Toy

Cement Mixer

(Put-ti, Put-ti)

Words and Music by Slim Gaillard and Lee Ricks

In this song by Slim Gaillard, nonsense words that resemble scat singing syllables tell about making concrete. The repetitive melody suggests the mixing of cement, and the repeated part with its jazzy rhythm makes the song fun to sing.

Not too fast

mf (snap fingers)

mf with plenty of vout

F Dm(7) Gm(7) C(7) F Dm(7)

6 5+ 6 1 6 5+ 6 1   6 5+ 6 1 6

Ce-ment mix-er! put – ti, put-ti,___   Ce-ment mix-er! put-

Gm(7) C(7) F Dm(7) Gm(7) C(7)

5+ 6 1   6 5+ 6 1 6 5+ 6 1

ti, put-ti,___   Ce-ment mix-er! put – ti, put-ti,___

F N.C.

1 2 4 6 8 1 2 4 6 9 1 4 6 8 8 1

A pud-dle o' voot-y, pud-dle o' goot-y, pud-dle o' scoot-y.

Cement Mixer (Put-ti, Put-ti)

122

BINGO

For all we know, there may have been a farmer with a dog named "Bingo." If there was, he probably came from Britain, because that is where this song originated. Traditionally, children sing all the letters in the name "Bingo" the first time. The second time, they clap on the letter "B" and sing "I-N-G-O." The third time, they clap "B-I" and sing "N-G-O." This continues until all of the letters are clapped rather than sung. Children have been playing this musical game for many years; maybe since 1780, when this song was first published.

Brightly, with humor

There was a farm-er who had a dog, And Bing-o was his name-o. B-I-N-G-O, B-I-N-G-O, B-I-N-G-O, And Bing-o was his name-o.

I Know an Old Lady

Words and Music by Alan Mills and Rose Bonne

Alan Mills (1914 – 77), who has been called the voice of Canadian folk music, left a 15-year career as a reporter to pursue his folksinging interests. He has made some two dozen records and toured extensively. Mills set "I Know an Old Lady" to music in 1951. This silly song about an old lady who had a most peculiar diet is a children's favorite. It has a surprise ending.

Moderately and somewhat freely

I Know an Old Lady

wrig-gled and wrig-gled and tick-led in-side her. She swal-lowed the spi-der to

catch the fly, But I don't know why she swal-lowed the fly. I guess she'll die!__ I

after last verse only

know an old la-dy who swal-lowed a horse. *(spoken)* She's dead, of course!

f with mock solemnity

whimsically

Words and Music by Tom Glazer

Tom Glazer is a well-known American balladeer and folksinger. He has performed on radio and television and plays concerts regularly. "On Top of Spaghetti" is among his best-loved recordings for children. This parody of the American folk song "On Top of Old Smoky" seems to have originated among schoolchildren in Westchester County, New York, where Glazer and his family live. He heard a version of it from his own children, rewrote it and published the song in 1963. Who on earth could possibly mind having a spaghetti-and-meatball tree in the backyard? Try not to laugh too hard while singing.

Moderately fast, with spirit

1. On top of spa - ghet - ti _____ All
(2) gar - den _____ And
(3) cov - ered _____ With

(1) cov - ered with cheese, _____ I lost my poor meat - ball _____
(2) un - der a bush, _____ And then my poor meat - ball _____
(3) beau - ti - ful moss; _____ It grew love - ly meat - balls _____

(1) _____ When some - bod - y sneezed. It rolled off the
(2) _____ Was noth - ing but mush. The mush was as
(3) _____ And to - ma - to sauce. So if you eat spa -

128

F   C

8 6   **6   4   5   6   5**   **1**
(1) ta - ble_____ And on - to the floor,_____ And
(2) tast - y_____ As   tast - y could be,_____ And
(3) ghet - ti_____ All cov - ered with cheese,_____ Hold

                                                                    ⌐1. 2.
G(7)   C   F

1   3   5   5   2   **3 (3) 4   3   2   1**
(1) then my poor meat-ball_____ Rolled   out of the door.
(2) ear-ly next sum-mer,_____ It grew in - to a tree.
(3) on to your meat-balls_____ And   don't ev - er

                                                                    ⌐3.
C   N.C.   C   F   C   N.C.

                        1   1   3   5   **1**
                        2. It rolled in the sneeze.   A - choo!
                        3. The tree was all

                                                    Slide up
                                                    white keys

                                                    Strike keyboard
                                                    with elbow

Mail Myself to You

Words and Music by Woody Guthrie

Woody Guthrie, an American folksinger of the 1930s and '40s, wrote hundreds of songs about his country, including "This Land Is Your Land" (see page 188). But he also wrote children's songs. Among them is this song that expresses an idea we have all probably thought of at one time. How nice it would be to mail yourself to someone you miss . . . and who misses you.

Fast and sassy

Lyrics with fingering numbers:

5 5 5 5 5 3 4 4 4 2 5 5 5 5 3 2 5 5
I'm a-gon-na wrap my-self in pa-per; I'm gon-na daub my-self with glue,

1 1 3 3 4 4 4 6 5 5 5 5 3 2 2 1
Stick some stamps on top of my head, I'm gon-na mail my-self to you.

5 5 5 5 5 5 3 3 3 2 2 5 5 5 5 3 2 1 2
I'm a-gon-na tie me up in a red string; I'm gon-na tie blue rib-bons too.

PUT YOUR FINGER IN THE AIR

Words and Music by Woody Guthrie

"Put Your Finger in the Air" is another very well-known children's song that was written by the legendary Woody Guthrie. Woody's son Arlo is also a folksinger, as well as an actor, and many of Woody's children's songs were probably written for him. Can you make up some new words for this one? Two more verses could be "Put your finger on your lips . . . So you won't make any slips . . ." and "Put your finger on your knee . . . And count up, one, two, three . . ."

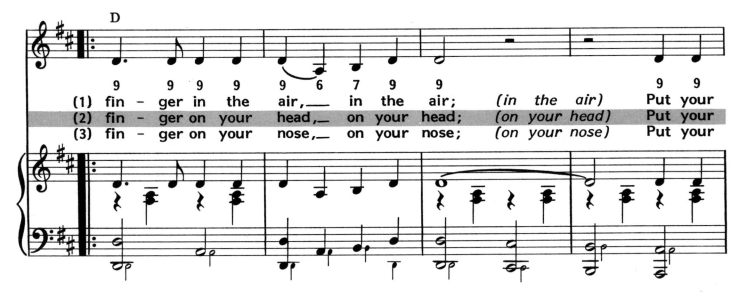

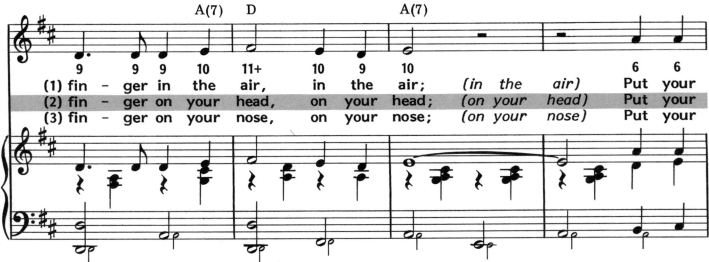

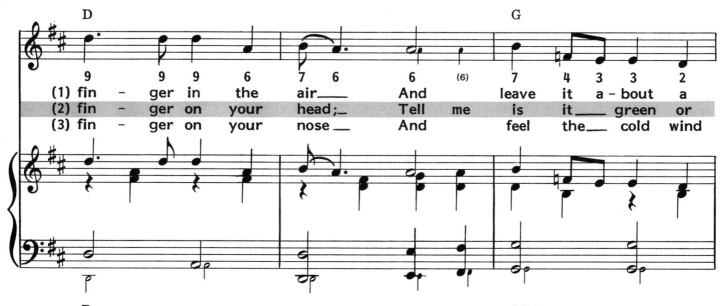

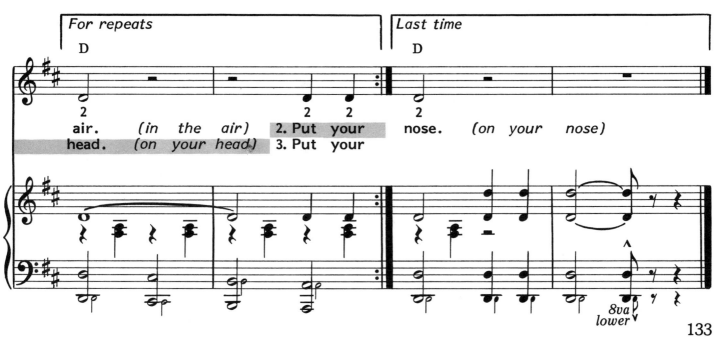

John Jacob Jingleheimer Schmidt

This is a traditional song, frequently sung by children at summer camp, about a person with an extraordinarily long name. It's kind of fun to say the name, too. Children love to sing this song as if it has no end. As soon as they get to the last "dah," they head straight back to the beginning and start again. This goes on until they get too tired to continue singing or some grownup nearby can stand no more . . . whichever comes first.

Brisk 4

John Ja-cob Jin-gle-hei-mer Schmidt, His name is my name too.

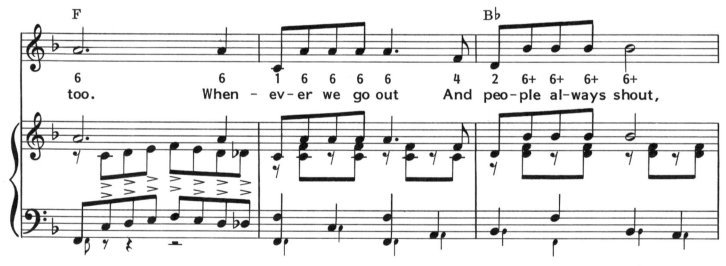

When-ev-er we go out And peo-ple al-ways shout,

"John Ja-cob Jin-gle-hei-mer Schmidt." Dah dah dah dah, Dah dah dah.

134

Barney Google

Words and Music by Billy Rose and Con Conrad

This song, based on the cartoon character of the same name, was written for comedian Eddie Cantor (who certainly had "goo-goo-googly" eyes), but it was the vaudeville team of Olsen and Johnson who made it a hit. It's difficult to imagine Barney Google putting Rudolf Valentino and Douglas Fairbanks — two of the leading men of the silent movies — to shame . . . but he did. That Barney Google was some guy!

Moderately

Lyrics:

Who's the most im - por - tant man this coun - try ev - er knew?
Who's the great - est lov - er that this coun - try ev - er knew?

Who's the man our pres - i - dents tell
Who's the man that Val - en - tin - o

135

*William Jennings Bryan, unsuccessful Democratic U.S. Presidential candidate in 1900 and 1908
**Charles Evans Hughes, Chief Justice, U.S. Supreme Court (1930 – 41)

MAIRZY DOATS

**Words and Music by Milton Drake,
Al Hoffman and Jerry Livingston**

Milton Drake got the idea for this song when he heard his four-year-old daughter recite a rhyme, slurring the words together as she spoke. If, as the song says, "the words sound queer and funny to your ear," see the middle of the song for the "translation."

Lightly, with a lilt

Mair – zy doats and do – zy doats and lid – dle lam – zy div – ey, A kid-dle-y div-ey too, would-n't you? Yes! mair-zy doats and do-zy doats and lid-dle lam-zy div-ey, A kid-dle-y div-ey too, would-n't you? If the

The Flat Foot Floogee

Words and Music by Slim Gaillard, Slam Stewart and Bud Green

Way back in the 1930s, this song grew out of some spontaneous playing-around by guitarist Slim Gaillard and bass fiddler Slam Stewart (Slim and Slam). It became popular because it has all the right ingredients: a swing rhythm, lots of repetition that makes it easy to learn and some puzzling words that are amusing to say. The only question is: How do you dance the Flat Foot Floogee? No one really knows, so make up your own steps and teach them to your family.

rhymes with "how"

(I Scream—You Scream—We All Scream for)

ICE CREAM

Words and Music by Howard Johnson, Billy Moll and Robert King

The Howard Johnson who is credited as one of the writers of this song is not the Howard Johnson of the many ice-cream flavors. As a matter of fact, back in 1927, when this song was written, exotic-flavored ice creams were unknown, and one probably had to settle for vanilla, chocolate, strawberry or maybe "sasparoola" (sarsaparilla). Johnson is best known for his popular spelling song "M-O-T-H-E-R, a word that means the world to me." For generations, children have chanted "I scream, you scream, we all scream for ice cream." Nobody knows which came first, the song or the chant.

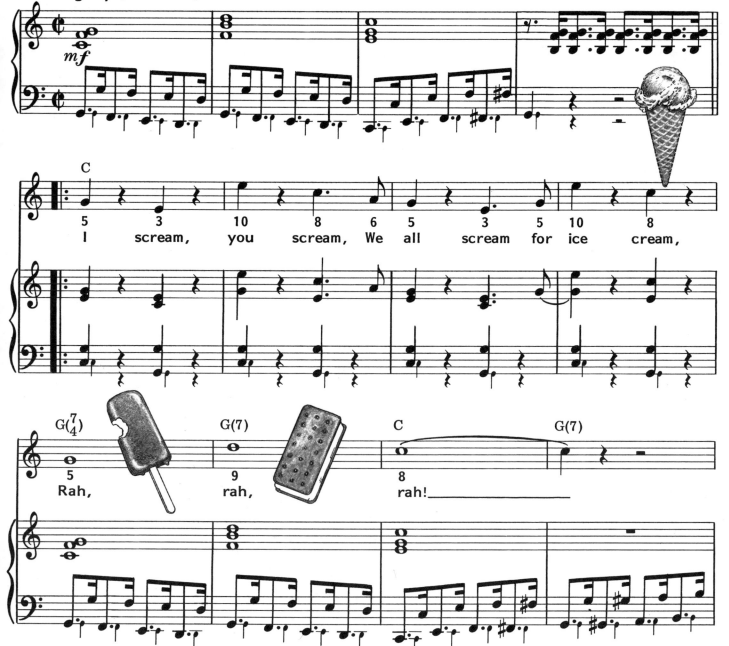

Brightly (♩ =1 beat)

I scream, you scream, We all scream for ice cream,

Rah, rah, rah!

(I Scream — You Scream — We All Scream for) Ice Cream

Tues - days, Mon - days, We all scream for
Frost - ed malt - ed Or pep - pered and

sun - daes, Siss, boom,
salt - ed, Siss, boom,

bah!_____ Boo - la, boo - la,_____
bah!_____ Oh, spu - mo - ni,_____

____ Sas - pa - roo - la,_____ If you've got
____ Oh, tor - to - ni_____ And, con - fi -

THE HUT-SUT SONG

Words and Music by Leo V. Killion, Ted McMichael and Jack Owens

Leo V. Killion, who worte the zany words of "The Hut-Sut Song," was an attorney for the California Legislative Council. We're sure that his arguments in court were a lot clearer than the make-believe-Swedish nonsense lyrics that he created. Freddy Martin and His Orchestra were the first to make the

song popular, in 1939. It was later heard in the movie *San Antonio Rose* (1941), in which it was sung by the group called The Merry Macs (another of the song's composers, Ted McMichael, was one of the Macs), and in *From Here to Eternity* (1953). It's just about time for a revival of this catchy tune.

Hut - sut

Rawl - son on the rill-er-ah And a braw-la, braw-la soo-it. Hut-sut

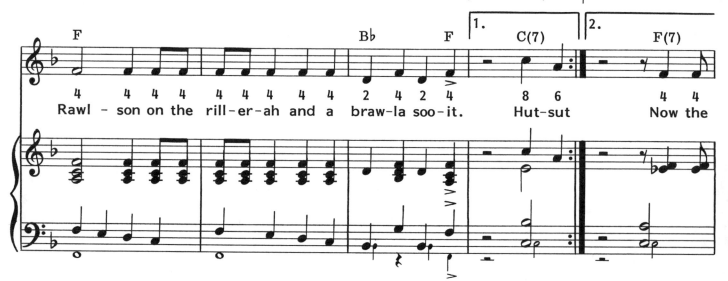

Rawl - son on the rill-er-ah and a braw-la soo-it. Hut-sut ... Now the

New version by Bill Lewis

It Ain't Gonna Rain No More

This song, probably based on a Southern folk tune, turns up every now and then with a new set of verses. There was a popular topical version in 1923, and it was sung in the film *Has Anybody Seen My Gal* (1952). It's time to enjoy it again, and here's a new version to help you do that.

Spirited

mf

F

6 5 4 4 4 6 6 4 4 1 1 4 4 4 3 4

1. Oh, it ain't gon-na rain no more, no more; It ain't gon-na rain no
(2) ain't gon-na rain no more, no more; It ain't gon-na rain no

C(7)

5 6+ 6+ 6+ 5 5 5 3 3 3 1 1 1

(1) more. Ain't gon-na snow and it ain't gon-na pour, Oh, it
(2) more. How in the heck can I wash my neck When it

1. F   **2.** F   **Fine** F

1 1 1 2 3 4 6 5 4 6 5 4

(1) ain't gon-na rain no more. 2.Oh, it
(2) ain't gon-na rain no more? 3.Oh, I you?

8va

148

5. (Oh, it) ain't gonna rain no more, no more;
   It ain't gonna rain no more.
   How in the dickens can I count my chickens
   If it ain't gonna rain no more?

6. Made a garden on my roof,
   Weeded every day.
   Prayed for rain, but when it came,
   It washed my roof away.

7. It ain't gonna rain no more, no more;
   It ain't gonna rain no more.
   Now I s'pose I can pick my rose;
   It ain't gonna rain no more.

8. Oh, it isn't going to rain anymore, anymore;
   It isn't going to rain anymore.
   The grammar's right, but it sure sounds trite,
   And what's more it's a bore.

9. Oh, it ain't gonna rain no more, no more;
   It ain't gonna rain no more.
   How in the deuce can I cook my goose
   If it ain't gonna rain no more?

10. Oh, I like to sing this silly song,
    Make up verses too.
    It's no offense if they don't make sense;
    I can, why can't you?

CAMPTOWN RACES

Words and Music by Stephen Foster

They called him "America's troubadour," the
first truly great American songwriter — Stephen Foster —
who in his short life wrote songs that were so well known and loved
that people referred to them as "folk songs." Like so many of Foster's
other songs, "Camptown Races" (originally called "Gwine to Run All
Night") was written to be sung in a minstrel show. But it wasn't long before it
became a favorite with people everywhere in North America. If you sing this
very lively dance tune, it will soon become one of your favorites, too.

Moderately

Camp-town la – dies sing their song, Doo – dah, doo – dah! The
long – tail fil-ly and the big black horse, Doo – dah, doo – dah! They

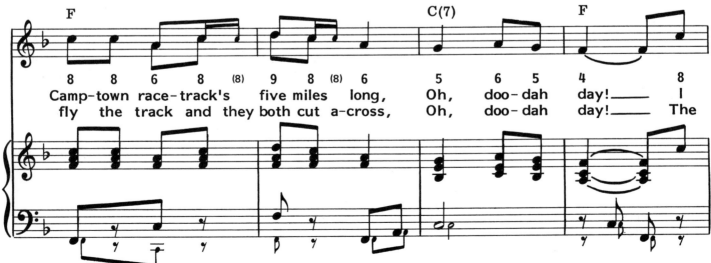

Camp-town race-track's five miles long, Oh, doo – dah day!___ I
fly the track and they both cut a-cross, Oh, doo – dah day!___ The

Father's Old Grey Whiskers

"Father's Old Grey Whiskers" was once a great favorite with college students. It undoubtedly hails from the turn of the century, when group singing was a national pastime. It has an endless number of verses, seven of them included here. Back in the early 1900s, when the song was popular, the older men were the ones with whiskers. Today it is the younger men who sport them.

Brightly

(1) have a dear old dad-dy For whom I night-ly pray. He
(2) round the sup-per ta-ble, We make a hap-py group, Un-
3. Fa-ther had a strong back; ___ Now it's all caved in. He

(1) has a set of whis-kers That are al-ways in the way.
(2) til dear fa-ther's whis-kers Get ___ tan-gled in the soup.
(3) stepped up-on his whis-kers And ___ walked up to his chin.

152

They're al-ways in the way; The cow eats them for hay. They hide the dirt on Dad-dy's shirt; They're al-ways in the way.

4. We have a dear old mother;
With him at night she sleeps.
She wakes up in the morning
Eating shredded wheat.
Chorus

5. We have a dear old brother;
He has a Ford machine.
He uses Father's whiskers
To strain the gasoline.
Chorus

6. Father fought in World War II;
He wasn't killed, you see.
He hid behind his whiskers
And fooled the enemy.
Chorus

7. Father in a tavern;
He likes his lager beer.
He pins a pretzel on his nose
To keep his whiskers clear.
Chorus

153

Words and Music by Saxie Dowell

"Three Little Fishies" is a novelty song that was popularized by Kay Kyser and His Orchestra in 1941, when that band was riding high in popularity as a result of the music-quiz radio program called *Kay Kyser's Kollege of Musical Knowledge*. The daffy little tune with its baby talk and nonsense words (a translation is provided) was a jukebox favorite and sold over a million records. The song has been around a long time, but you don't have to dust it off. An amazing number of children know and love it.

THREE LITTLE FISHIES
(Itty Bitty Poo)

Three Little Fishies (Itty Bitty Poo)

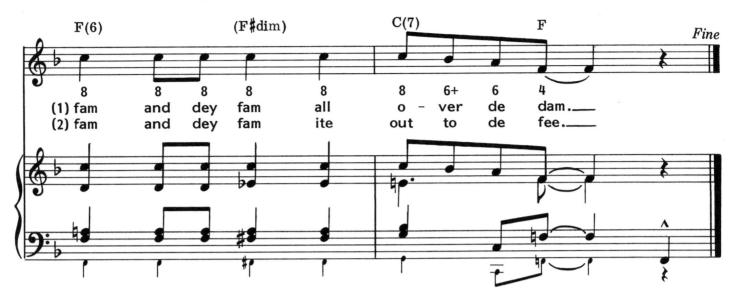

8   8   8   8   8   8   6+   6   4
(1) fam and dey fam all o - ver de dam.___
(2) fam and dey fam ite out to de fee.___

Interlude

3. "Whee!" elled de itty fitties, "Ears a wot of fun.
Ee'll fim in de fee ill de day is un."
Dey fam and dey fam, and it was a wark,
Till aw of a tudden dey taw a tark!

*"Whee!" yelled the little fishies, "Here's a lot of fun.
We'll swim in the sea till the day is done."
They swam and they swam, and it was a lark,
Till all of a sudden they saw a shark!*

Boop boop dit-tem dot-tem what-tem Chu!
Boop boop dit-tem dot-tem what-tem Chu!
Boop boop dit-tem dot-tem what-tem Chu!
Till aw of a tudden dey taw a tark!

4. "He'p!" tied de itty fitties, "Dee! ook at all de fales!"
And twit as dey tood, dey turned on deir tails!
And bat to de poo in de meddy dey fam,
And dey fam and dey fam bat over de dam.

*"Help!" cried the little fishies, "Gee! look at all the whales!"
And quick as they could, they turned on their tails.
And back to the pool in the meadow they swam,
And they swam and they swam back over the dam.*

Boop boop dit-tem dot-tem what-tem Chu!
Boop boop dit-tem dot-tem what-tem Chu!
Boop boop dit-tem dot-tem what-tem Chu!
And dey fam and dey fam bat over de dam.

156

This song was written for Frances White, who introduced it in the Florenz Ziegfeld revue *Midnight Frolics* way back in 1916, and it was used again two years later in a revue called *Hitchy-Koo*. The inspiration for the song probably did not result from the difficulty of spelling the name of the river and the state, but rather from the fun of saying "M-I-S-S-I-S-S-I-P-P-I." As a result of the song's popularity, almost everybody can spell Mississippi correctly.

M-I-S-S-I-S-S-I-P-P-I

Words by Bert Hanlon and Benny Ryan; Music by Harry Tierney

I'VE BEEN WORKING ON THE RAILROAD

"I've Been Working on the Railroad," a work song probably sung by the men who laid the countless miles of track that finally stretched from coast to coast, is actually two songs strung together — the link being the name Dinah. ("Someone's in the Kitchen with Dinah" is an old minstrel-show song.) In 1894 it was published as "Levee Song," possibly because its catchy tune and rhythm were taken up by men who worked along the river banks.

Very steady, like a march

I've been work-ing on the rail - road All the live - long day.

I've been work-ing on the rail - road To pass the time of day.

Don't you hear the whis-tle blow - ing? Rise up so ear-ly in the morn.

158

Don't you hear the cap-tain shout - ing, "Di - nah, blow your horn"?

Faster

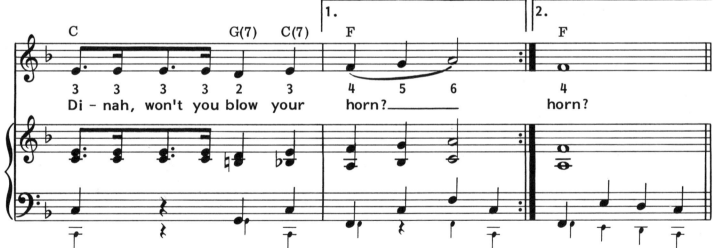

Di - nah, won't you blow, Di - nah, won't you blow,

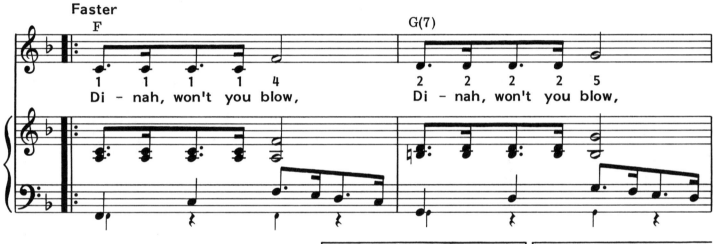

Di - nah, won't you blow your horn?_____ horn?

Some-one's in the kitch-en with Di - nah; Some-one's in the kitch-en I

PUFF
(The Magic Dragon)

**Words and Music by
Peter Yarrow and Leonard Lipton**

Peter Yarrow, one of the writers of this song, is the Peter of Peter, Paul and Mary, the group that delighted millions with their special blend of voices interpreting songs in the contemporary folk-song style. "Puff" is not just an amusing song for children; it is also a song about growing up and about the loss of childhood's beautiful innocence. No wonder it soared to the top of the popular music charts in 1963. The story of little Jackie Paper, frolicking with the friendly dragon Puff, remains a favorite today.

1. Puff, the mag-ic drag-on, lived by the sea And
(2) geth-er they would trav-el on a boat with bil-lowed sail; —
(3) drag-on lives for-ev-er but not so lit-tle boys; —
(4) head was bent in sor-row; green scales fell like rain. —

(1) frol-icked in the au-tumn mist in a land called Ho-nah-Lee.
(2) Jack-ie kept a look-out perched on Puff's gi-gan-tic tail.
(3) Paint-ed wings and gi-ant rings make way for oth-er toys.
(4) Puff no long-er went to play a-long the cher-ry lane. With-

Puff (The Magic Dragon)

C   Em   F   C

8   8   8   8   7   5   (5) (5)   6   6   8   8   5   5

(1) Lit – tle   Jack – ie   Pa – per   loved   that   ras – cal   Puff   And
(2) No – ble   kings   and   prin – ces   would   bow   when–e'er   they   came;   —
(3) One   grey   night   it   hap–pened,   Jack–ie   Pa – per   came   no   more,   And
(4) out   his   life–long   friend,—   Puff   could   not   be   brave,   So

F   C   Am   D(7)   G(7)   C   G(7)

4   4   5   4   3   5   8   (8)   8   6   8   7   9   8   7

(1) brought   him   strings   and   seal – ing   wax   and   oth – er   fan – cy   stuff.   Oh!
(2) Pi – rate   ships   would   low'r   their   flag   when   Puff   roared   out   his   name.   Oh!
(3) Puff   that   might – y   drag – on,   He   ceased   his   fear–less   roar.   Oh!
(4) Puff   that   might – y   drag – on   sad–ly   slipped   in – to   his   cave.   Oh!

C   Em   F   C

8   8   8   8   7   5   6   8   8   5   5

Puff,   the   mag – ic   drag – on,   lived   by   the   sea   And

162

frol-icked in the au-tumn mist in a land called Ho-nah - Lee.

Puff, the mag - ic drag - on, lived by the sea And

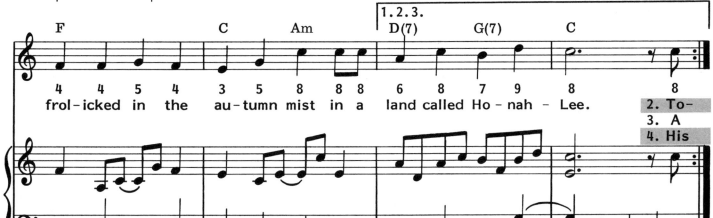

1.2.3.

frol-icked in the au-tumn mist in a land called Ho-nah - Lee.

2. To-
3. A
4. His

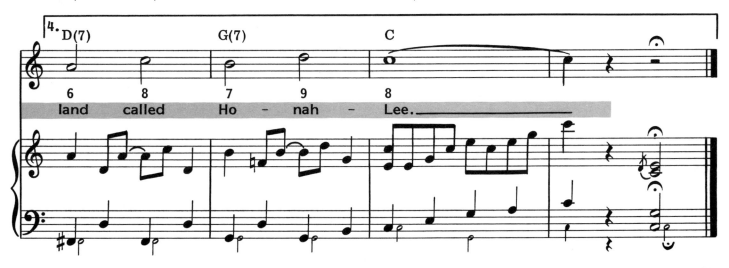

4.

land called Ho - nah - Lee.

CLEMENTINE

The authorship of the song "Clementine" is rather cloudy. The words first were credited to H. S. Thompson in 1863, and then, 20 years later, Percy Montrose was given credit for both the words and the music. However, we should be thankful to whoever is responsible for this nonsensical song about a gold miner's daughter. It has provided countless hours of enjoyment for campers, schoolchildren and other folks who have all loved singing about poor Clementine, "lost and gone forever."

Moderately

1. In a

F

(1) cav - ern, in a can - yon, Ex - ca -
(2) was and like a fair - y, And her
(3) duck - lings to the wa - ter Ev - 'ry
(4) lips a - bove the wa - ter Blow - ing

C(7)   Gm   C(7)

(1) vat - ing for a mine, Dwelt a min - er, for - ty-
(2) shoes___ were num - ber nine, Her - ring box - es with - out
(3) morn - ing just at nine, Hit her foot a - gainst a
(4) bub - bles soft and fine, But, a - las, I was no

164

Chorus
(1) nin - er, And his daugh - ter Clem - en - tine.
(2) top - ses, San - dals were for Clem - en - tine.
(3) splin - ter, Fell in - to the foam - ing brine.
(4) swim - mer, So I lost my Clem - en - tine.
Oh, my
dar - ling, Oh, my dar - ling, Oh, my dar - ling Clem - en -
tine, You are lost and gone for - ev - er, Dread - ful
sor - ry, Clem - en - tine.
1.2.3.
2. Light she
3. Drove she
4. Ru - by
4.
tine.

Little Brown Jug

This ode to the very invigorating contents of the "Little Brown Jug" was first published in 1869 and attributed to R. A. Eastburn, a pseudonym for Joseph E. Winner. (Winner was the brother of Septimus Winner, who wrote "Oh Where, Oh Where Has My Little Dog Gone?" and "Ten Little Indians.") Apparently the song had been sung in different versions since early in the 19th century, and Winner only claimed that the "jug" was "put into shape and filled up" by him. In 1939, Glenn Miller and His Orchestra revived the song with such success that over a million records of it were sold. It may not have been chocolate milk that Winner put in the "jug," but children have always enjoyed singing this song, especially the chorus — a great knee-bouncer for infants.

Brightly, like a polka

My

wife and I lived all a - lone, In a
you who makes my friends and foes; 'Tis___

lit - tle log hut we called our own. She loved gin and
you___ who makes me wear old clothes. Here you are so

167

Ha, Ha, This-a-Way

Words and Music by Huddie Ledbetter;
Collected and adapted by John A. Lomax and Alan Lomax

This is probably the original version of the song as sung by the great blues singer Huddie ("Leadbelly") Ledbetter, and it is doubtlessly autobiographical. There are many versions of the song, most of which call for some action to be done on the "Ha, ha, this-a-way." You can add more verses and make up actions for the chorus. ("When I was a cowboy, a cowboy, a cowboy" . . . with a bouncing cowboy "motion" on "Ha, ha, this-a-way.")

Brightly

Chorus

Ha, ha, this - a - way, Ha, ha, that - a - way,
Hi, this - a - way, Hi, that - a - way,

Ha, ha, this - a - way, Then, oh, then.
Hi, this - a - way, Then, oh, then.

Last time end here

1. When I was a lit-tle boy, lit-tle boy, lit-tle boy,
2. Mom-ma came an' got me, got me, got me;
3. Pa-pa drank whis-key, whis-key, whis-key;

4. I went to school, went to school, went to school, boys,
   I went to school when I was twelve years old.
   Obeyed the rules, the rules, the rules, boy,
   Obeyed the rules as I was told.
   Chorus

5. Learned my lesson, lesson, lesson,
   Learned my lesson as I was tol'.
   Wasn't that a blessin', blessin', blessin'?
   Wasn't that a blessin' to save my soul?
   Chorus

6. Liked my teacher, teacher, teacher,
   Liked my teacher, so I was tol'.
   Prayed like a preacher, preacher, preacher,
   Prayed like a preacher to save my soul.
   Chorus

7. I went to school, went to school, went to school;
   I went to school when I was twelve years old.
   Teacher didn't whiff me, whiff me, whiff me;
   Teacher didn't whiff me to save my soul.
   Chorus

The Grey Goose

Words and Music by Huddie Ledbetter

Collected and adapted by John A. Lomax and Alan Lomax

HONK!

Although credited to Huddie Ledbetter, "The Grey Goose" probably dates back to the days of slavery and represents the resiliency of the Negro slave. No amount of oppression could destroy him, for he possessed the same toughness and spirit as the grey goose. Like so many other songs, "The Grey Goose" was collected by Library of Congress folk-song archivist John A. Lomax and his son Alan. The song was sung by black convicts in Texas, who performed it in call-and-response fashion: one man sang the narrative and the others responded with "Lord, Lord, Lord." If you can think of another way that the goose got everyone's goat, try creating your own verse for the song.

Brightly

N.C.   Eb   Bb   C

4	5+	5	4	2+	4	5	6+	8	(8)	(8)
1. Preach-er	went	a-	hunt-	in',		Lord,	Lord,	Lord.		
2. Car-ried	'long	his	shot-	gun,		Lord,	Lord,	Lord.		
3. 'Long___	came	a	grey	goose,		Lord,	Lord,	Lord.		
4. Gun___	went	a-	boo-	loo,		Lord,	Lord,	Lord.		
5. Down___	came	a	grey	goose,		Lord,	Lord,	Lord.		
(6) six___	weeks	a-	fall-	in',		Lord,	Lord,	Lord.	He	was
(7) gave	a	feath-er-	pick-	in',		Lord,	Lord,	Lord.	Then	they
8. Your___	wife	an'	my	wife,		Lord,	Lord,	Lord.	___	
(9) six___	weeks	a-	pick-	in',		Lord,	Lord,	Lord.	They	was
(11) won-der	what's	the	mat-	ter,		Lord,	Lord,	Lord.	Well,	I
(12) put	him	on	to	par-	boil,	Lord,	Lord,	Lord.	So	they
(13) six___	weeks	a-	boil-	in',		Lord,	Lord,	Lord.	He	was
(14) put	him	on	the	ta-	ble,	Lord,	Lord,	Lord.	So	they
15. Fork___	could-n't	stick	him,			Lord,	Lord,	Lord.	___	
16. Knife___	could-n't	cut	him,			Lord,	Lord,	Lord.	___	
(18) took	him	to	the	hog	pen,	Lord,	Lord,	Lord.	So	they
19. Broke	the	sow's___	teeth	out,		Lord,	Lord,	Lord.	___	

Rock Island Line

Words and Music by Paul Campbell and Joel Newman

This song has truly been through the "folk process." The American folklorist Alan Lomax heard "Rock Island Line" sung by a convict named Kelly Pace at the Cumins State Prison Farm in Gould, Arkansas. Pace recorded it for Lomax in 1934, Huddie Ledbetter adapted it, The Weavers recorded it . . . and this version, recorded by England's Lonnie Donegan Skiffle Group, became a hit in this country in 1956. The Rock Island Line doesn't run anymore, but you can pretend you're riding the railroad as you sing this song. And no ticket is needed.

Polly-Wolly-Doodle

"Polly-Wolly-Doodle" started out as a Civil War minstrel song and was popularized after the war by minstrel star Billy Emerson. It was used as a "walk-around," the finale in which each performer would step forward to sing a verse, after which the entire company would sing the final chorus while clapping, stamping and dancing.

Brightly, with humor

1. Oh, I went down South for to see my Sal, Sing
(2) Sal she is a maid-en fair, Sing
(3) grass-hop-per sit-tin' on a rail-road track, Sing

(1) pol-ly-wol-ly-doo-dle all the day. My Sal-ly is a
(2) pol-ly-wol-ly-doo-dle all the day. With curl-y eyes and
(3) pol-ly-wol-ly-doo-dle all the day. A-pick-in' his teeth with a

(1) spunk-y gal, Sing pol-ly-wol-ly-doo-dle all the day.
(2) laugh-ing hair, Sing pol-ly-wol-ly-doo-dle all the day.
(3) car-pet tack, Sing pol-ly-wol-ly-doo-dle all the day.

Fare thee

4. Oh, I went to bed, but it wasn't no use,
Sing polly-wolly-doodle all the day.
My feet stuck out like a chicken roost,
Sing polly-wolly-doodle all the day.
Chorus

5. Behind the barn down on my knees,
Sing polly-wolly-doodle all the day.
I thought I heard a chicken sneeze,
Sing polly-wolly-doodle all the day.
Chorus

6. He sneezed so hard with the whooping cough,
Sing polly-wolly-doodle all the day.
He sneezed his head and tail right off,
Sing polly-wolly-doodle all the day.
Chorus

If You're Happy and You Know It
(Clap Your Hands)

What do you do when you're happy? Smile? Laugh? This song will give you a chance to sing and move around if you're happy. You could make up your own verses, depending on how you feel. For example: "If you're

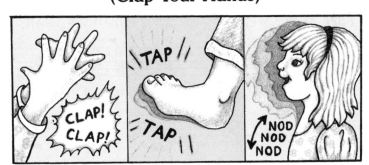

(supply word) and you know it, touch the floor"; "If you're *(supply word)* and you know it, stamp your feet." Suppose you were sad. What words could you sing to this song? What do you *do* when you're sad?

Like a slow march, in 2 (♩.=1 beat)

1. If you're hap-py and you know it, clap your hands. *(clap, clap)* If you're hap-py and you
2. If you're hap-py and you know it, tap your toe. *(tap, tap)* If you're hap-py and you
3. If you're hap-py and you know it, nod your head. *(nod, nod)* If you're hap-py and you

(1) know it, clap your hands. *(clap, clap)* If you're hap-py and you know it, Then your
(2) know it, tap your toe. *(tap, tap)* If you're hap-py and you know it, Then your
(3) know it, nod your head. *(nod, nod)* If you're hap-py and you know it, Then your

(1) face will sure-ly show it; If you're hap-py and you know it, clap your hands. *(clap, clap)*
(2) face will sure-ly show it; If you're hap-py and you know it, tap your toe. *(tap, tap)*
(3) face will sure-ly show it; If you're hap-py and you know it, nod your head. *(nod, nod)*

176

John Brown's Baby

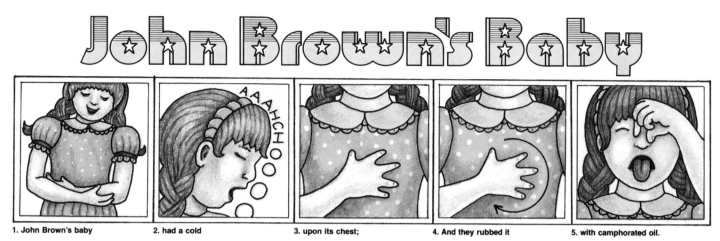

1. John Brown's baby   2. had a cold   3. upon its chest;   4. And they rubbed it   5. with camphorated oil.

"John Brown's Baby" is a parody of the Civil War song "John Brown's Body." When singing it, you first sing the song through. Then you sing it five times more, each time omitting a different key word and substituting the pantomimed action for it as shown in the illustrations above. Therefore, each time the song is sung through, the actions are repeated instead of the words, until finally there are five actions replacing six words.

SHE'LL BE COMIN' ROUND THE MOUNTAIN

New words by Paul and Dan Fox

"She'll Be Comin' Round the Mountain" is based on a Negro spiritual, "When the Chariot Comes." In *The American Songbag,* author Carl Sandburg reports that mountaineers sang the spiritual and turned it into this joyful song. Then, railroad work gangs in the Midwest picked it up in the 1890s. Whatever its origins, the song has always been a great favorite. Sing it now, with new verses by arranger Dan Fox and his son Paul.

D(7) ... **G**

6
(1) comes.＿＿＿ She'll be com - in' round the moun-tain; She'll be
(2) comes.＿＿＿ She'll be rid - in' on a cam - el Or some
(3) comes.＿＿＿ She'll be tug - gin' on two tur - tles; They'll be
(4) comes.＿＿＿ She'll be carv - in' three thick this - tles Just to

9 8 7 7 7 7 6 5 5 5

C ... **D(7)**

3 3 3 3 6 5 4+ 3 2 2 2 2
(1) com - in' round the moun - tain; She'll be com - in' round the
(2) oth - er man - gy mam - mal; She'll be rid - in' on a
(3) wear - in' pur - ple gir - dles; She'll be tug - gin' on two
(4) make some pen - ny whis - tles; She'll be carv - in' three thick

G ... *For additional verses* | *Last time*
D(7)

7 6 3 4+ 5 2 3
(1) moun-tain when she comes.＿＿＿ 2. She'll be
(2) cam - el when she comes.＿＿＿ 3. She'll be
(3) tur - tles when she comes.＿＿＿ 4. She'll be
(4) this - tles when she comes.＿＿＿ 5. She'll be

There's even more! Turn to the next page for additional verses. 179

5. (She'll be) pluckin' four fat pheasants when she comes;
   She'll be pluckin' four fat pheasants when she comes.
   She'll be pluckin' four fat pheasants
   To give as Christmas presents;
   She'll be pluckin' four fat pheasants when she comes.

6. She'll be feedin' five fast foxes when she comes;
   She'll be feedin' five fast foxes when she comes.
   She'll be feedin' five fast foxes,
   Eatin' fast food in five boxes;
   She'll be feedin' five fast foxes when she comes.

7. She'll hold six scary spiders when she comes;
   She'll hold six scary spiders when she comes.
   First, a small one sat beside her,
   Then the others tried to bite her;
   Now she's holdin' no more spiders when she comes.

8. She'll send seven stingin' starfish when she comes;
   She'll send seven stingin' starfish when she comes.
   She'll send seven stingin' starfish;
   Did you know that starfish are fish?
   She'll send seven stingin' starfish when she comes.

9. She'll ride eight overweight elephants when she comes;
   She'll ride eight overweight elephants when she comes.
   She'll ride eight overweight elephants;
   How she got 'em is just irrelevance;
   She'll ride eight overweight elephants when she comes.

10. She'll be herdin' nine fine swine when she comes;
    She'll be herdin' nine fine swine when she comes.
    She'll be herdin' nine fine swine,
    Snout to nose in one straight line;
    She'll be herdin' nine fine swine when she comes.

11. She'll be ticklin' ten tan terriers when she comes;
    She'll be ticklin' ten tan terriers when she comes.
    She'll be ticklin' ten tan terriers;
    Come along, the more the merrier;
    She'll be ticklin' ten tan terriers when she comes.

12. Oh, we'll all go down to meet her when she comes;
    Oh, we'll all go down to meet her when she comes.
    Oh, we'll all go down to meet her;
    Oh, we'll all go down to greet her;
    Oh, we'll all go down to meet her when she comes.

This nursery rhyme, which was first sung in England and later in the Appalachian Mountain region of the United States, is now very well known everywhere in the country. Try changing the first line and seeing if you can keep going with new rhymes. One new version could be "Hush, little baby, don't make a peep; / Daddy's gonna buy you a small white sheep. / If that small white sheep don't 'baa,' /*(supply the rest of the rhyme)*."

Hush, Little Baby

Gentle lullaby

(no organ pedals on this song)

F   Bb   C(7)

1   6   6   6   6+   6   5   5   5

1. Hush, lit - tle ba - by, don't say a word;
2. If that mock - ing - bird don't__ sing,
3. If that dia - mond ring gets__ broke,

For additional words   F

Final ending   F

1   1   5   5   5   5   6   5   4   4   5   4   4   4

(1) Ma-ma's gon-na buy you a mock - ing - bird.
(2) Ma-ma's gon-na buy you a dia - mond ring.
(3) Ma-ma's gon-na buy you a bil - ly goat.

ba - by in town.

8va--

4. If that billy goat don't pull,
 Mama's gonna buy you a cart 'n' bull.

5. If that cart 'n' bull turn over,
 Mama's gonna buy you a dog named Rover.

6. If that dog named Rover don't bark,
 Mama's gonna buy you a horse 'n' cart.

7. If that horse 'n' cart fall down,
 You'll be the sweetest little baby in town.

A Frog Went A-Courtin'

There are various well-known versions of this song, and all of them can be traced to England. One version is possibly 400 years old. It is said that the frog refers to the Duke of Anjou (Anjou is an old French province) and the mouse to Queen Elizabeth I. If this is so, it might explain the reference to France in the last verse. This story song, popular since Colonial times, is fun to act out. All you need are two friends willing to help play the parts.

Moderate amphibian tempo

1. A

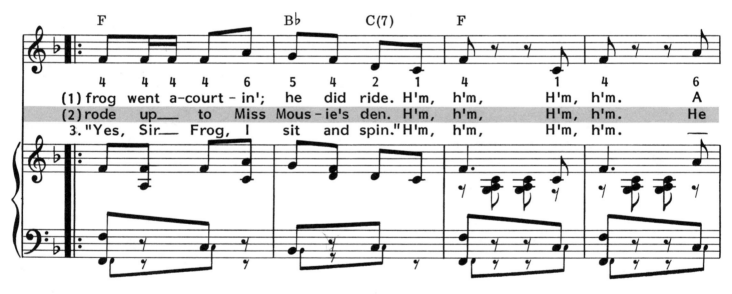

F   B♭   C(7)   F

(1) frog went a-court-in'; he did ride. H'm, h'm, H'm, h'm. A
(2) rode up__ to Miss Mous-ie's den. H'm, h'm, H'm, h'm. He
3. "Yes, Sir__ Frog, I sit and spin." H'm, h'm, H'm, h'm. __

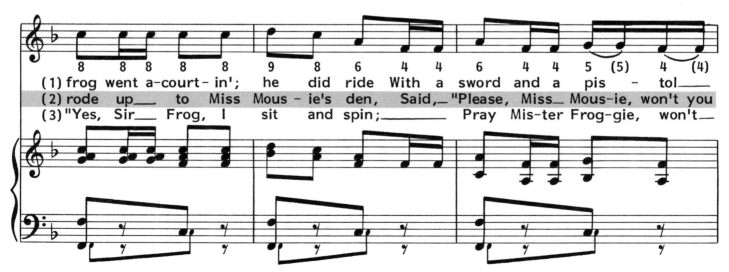

(1) frog went a-court-in'; he did ride With a sword and a pis - tol__
(2) rode up__ to Miss Mous-ie's den, Said,__ "Please, Miss__ Mous-ie, won't you
(3) "Yes, Sir__ Frog, I sit and spin;__ Pray Mis-ter Frog-gie, won't__

4. The frog said, "My dear, I've come to see."
   H'm, h'm,
   H'm, h'm.
   The frog said, "My dear, I've come to see
   If you, Miss Mousie, will marry me."
   H'm, h'm,
   H'm, h'm.

5. "I don't know what to say to that."
   H'm, h'm,
   H'm, h'm.
   "I don't know what to say to that
   Till I speak with my Uncle Rat."
   H'm, h'm,
   H'm, h'm.

6. When Uncle Rat came riding home.
   H'm, h'm,
   H'm, h'm.
   When Uncle Rat came riding home,
   Said he, "Who's been here since I've been gone?"
   H'm, h'm,
   H'm, h'm.

7. "A fine young froggie has been here."
   H'm, h'm,
   H'm, h'm.
   "A fine young froggie has been here;
   He means to marry me it's clear."
   H'm, h'm,
   H'm, h'm.

8. So Uncle Rat, he rode to town.
   H'm, h'm,
   H'm, h'm.
   So Uncle Rat, he rode to town
   And bought his niece a wedding gown.
   H'm, h'm,
   H'm, h'm.

9. The frog and mouse they went to France.
   H'm, h'm,
   H'm, h'm.
   The frog and mouse they went to France,
   And that's the end of my romance.
   H'm, h'm,
   H'm, h'm.

Old Dan Tucker

As you may have noticed, a few songs from minstrel shows became so popular that they were sung nationally and, just like folk songs, changed through oral tradition. One of these songs was "Old Dan Tucker," written by Dan Emmett, who, with three other entertainers, organized the first full-length minstrel show. Emmett also wrote the song "Dixie." "Old Dan Tucker" has been used as a square-dance song in New England, a play-party in the Southwest and a popular banjo tune just about everywhere. That Dan Tucker sure stirred things up when he came to town!

Brightly, like a square dance

1. I come to town the oth-er night; I heard the noise and saw the__ fight. The watch-man was a-run-nin'__ roun', Cry-in' "Old Dan Tuck-er's__ come to__ town." } So

2. Old Dan, he went down to the mill To get some meal to put in the swill. The mill-er__ swore by the point of his knife, He__ nev-er seen such a man in his life. } So

184

get out the way for Old Dan Tuck-er; Get out the way for Old Dan Tuck-er;

Get out the way for Old Dan Tuck-er; He's too late to come for sup-per.

3. Old Dan Tucker, he got drunk;
   He fell in the fire and he kicked up a chunk.
   A red-hot coal rolled in his shoe,
   And good Lord, boys, how the ashes flew.
   Chorus

4. Old Dan Tucker was a fine old man,
   Washed his face in a frying pan,
   Combed his hair with a wagon wheel,
   Died with a toothache in his heel.
   Chorus

RIDE A COCK-HORSE

It is commonly thought that the woman on the horse referred to in this nursery rhyme is either Queen Elizabeth I (she certainly shows up in a number of rhymes, doesn't she?) or the long-haired Lady Godiva. The "bells on her toes" may refer to a 15th-century style in which ladies sewed bells onto the toe of each shoe. The rocking rhythm of "Ride a Cock-Horse" seems to suggest a toy rocking horse rather than a real one. A rocking horse can't really take you too far, but your imagination should be able to take you anywhere you want to go.

Allegretto, with spirit (in 2, ♪. =1 beat)

Ride a cock-horse to Ban-bu-ry Cross To see a fine la-dy up-on a white horse, Rings on her fin-gers and bells on her toes; She shall have mu-sic wher-ev-er she goes.

This old English singing game has nothing to do with the animals called weasels. The "weasel" that goes "pop" may have been a tool used by English hatters, tailors and cobblers. When money was in short supply, they "popped," or pawned, their weasels.

With spirit, in 2 (♩.=1 beat)

All a-round the cob - bler's bench, The mon-key chased the wea - sel. The
Ru - fus has the whoop-ing cough, And Sal - ly has the meas - les, And

mon-key thought 'twas all___ in fun, }
that's the way the doc - tor goes, } Pop! goes the wea - sel. A

pen - ny for a spool___ of thread, A pen - ny for___ a nee - dle.

That's the way the mon - ey goes, Pop! goes the wea - sel.

THIS LAND IS YOUR LAND

**Words and
Music by Woody Guthrie**

This is probably the best-known and best-loved song of America's balladeer of the 1930s and '40s, Woody Guthrie. He sang of his country and its people, and he performed with the likes of Pete Seeger, Huddie ("Leadbelly") Ledbetter and Cisco Houston. He is regarded as one of the best writers of songs in contemporary folk-song style. All told, he wrote some 1,000 songs and influenced generations of folk-song writers and singers.

With spirit (♩=1 beat)

1. This land is

(1) your land;___ This land is my land.___ From Cal-i-
(2) walk-ing___ that rib-bon of high-way,___ I saw a-
(3) ram-bled,___ and I fol-lowed my foot-steps___ To the spark-ling
(4) shin-ing___ and I was stroll-ing,___ And the wheat fields
(5) liv-ing___ can ev-er stop me___ As I go

(1) for-nia___ to the New York Is-land,___ From the red-wood
(2) bove me___ that___ end-less sky-way;___ I___ saw be-
(3) sands of her dia-mond des-erts,___ And___ all a-
(4) wav-ing___ and the dust clouds roll-ing,___ As the fog was
(5) walk-ing___ that___ free-dom high-way. No-bod-y

Be Kind to Your Web-Footed Friends

This amusing song was popularized by Mitch Miller on his *Sing Along with Mitch* TV show. If the tune sounds familiar, it's because you've heard it before as "Stars and Stripes Forever," by John Philip Sousa.

**Words and Music by
Terry Gilkyson, Richard Dehr
and Frank Miller**

"Marianne" is one of the best-known calypso songs in the world. This adaptation from a West Indian folk song was popularized in 1957 by Terry Gilkyson and The Easy Riders, who turned it into a million-seller

recording. Gilkyson wrote the song with Frank Miller and Richard Dehr (The Easy Riders on the disc). It has been suggested that the "sand" Marianne was "sifting" was men . . . but, since she was so lovely and admired by all, who could possibly refrain from singing her praises? Try clapping a calypso beat while performing this saucy little song.

Moderate calypso tempo

mf

F   C(7)

1   6   6   6   1   6   6   6   6   5   6+   6   5

1. Mar – i – anne, oh, Mar – i – anne, oh, won't you mar – ry me?
2. When she walks a – long the shore, peo – ple pause to greet.
3. When we mar – ry, we will have a time you nev – er saw.

       F

1   5   5   5   1   5   5   5   5   6+   6   (6)   5   4

(1) We can have a bam – boo hut and bran – dy in the tea.
(2) White birds fly a – round her; lit – tle fish come to her feet.
(3) I will be so hap – py, I will kiss my moth – er – in – law. *(phooey!)*

Marianne

Bb

1 6 6 6   1 6 6 6   8 6+ 9 8   6+

(1) Leave your fat old ma – ma home; she nev – er will say yes.
(2) In her heart is love, but I'm the on – ly mor – tal man
(3) Chil – dren by the doz – en in and out the bam – boo hut,

C(7)   F   (F#dim) C(7)   F   *(spoken)*

9 9 10 9   8   8   6+ (6+) 8 6

(1) If Ma – ma don't know now, she can guess. *My, my, yes.*
(2) Who's al – lowed to kiss my Mar – i – anne. *Don't rush me.*
(3) One for ev – 'ry palm tree and cok – y – nut. *Hur – ry up now.*

Chorus

F   C(7)

6 8 4 6   6 5 6+

All day, all night, Mar – i – anne,_____

192

Down by the sea - side sift-in' sand.

E - ven lit - tle chil - dren love Mar - i - anne,

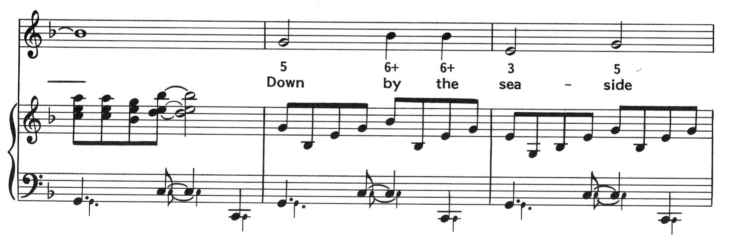

Down by the sea - side

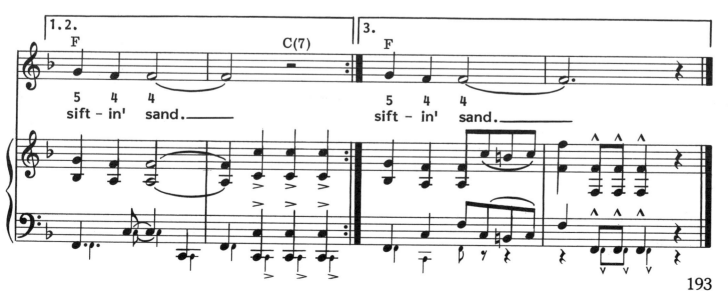

1.2. sift - in' sand.   3. sift - in' sand.

193

Alouette

Many a child has learned his or her first French by way of "Alouette." Little do they realize that "alouette" means "lark" and that the singer threatens the poor bird with plucking its feathers out . . . first from its head, then its beak, its nose, etc. Traditionally, the song is sung so that each portion of the unlucky bird that has already been named in a verse is repeated after each new part is added.

Allegretto (not fast, in 2; ♩=1 beat)

Oh, A - lou - et - te, gen - tille A - lou - et - te;
A - lou - et - te, je te plu - me - rai.
A - lou - et - te, gen - tille A - lou - et - te;

194   *For pronunciation, see page 28 of the lyric booklet.*

*Each chorus adds a new part of the body, in reverse order. For example, Chorus 3 is sung:

Et le nez, et le nez,
Et le bec, et le bec,
Et la têt', et le têt',
Alouett', Alouett'.
Oh, *etc.*

2. le bec *(beak)*
3. le nez *(nose)*
4. les yeux *(eyes)*
5. le cou *(neck)*

6. les ailes *(wings)*
7. le dos *(back)*
8. les pattes *(feet)*
9. la queue *(tail)*

Cockles and Mussels

"Cockles and Mussels" is a picturesque description of a vendor from the 18th century calling her wares in the streets of Dublin, Ireland. She was selling shellfish: cockles and mussels that she had probably harvested. North Americans are familiar with mussels. But cockles — small, clamlike mollusks — are found only in Europe and were plentiful on the beaches near Dublin. Molly Malone's plaintive cry became well known outside her native country in the 1950s, thanks in part to a recording by Burl Ives. The actual call of such women as Molly might have sounded a great deal like the "cockles and mussels" part of this song.

Gently

1. In
2. She
3. She

(1) Dub - lin's fair cit - y, Where girls are so pret - ty, 'Twas
(2) was a fish - mon - ger, But sure 'twas no won - der, For
(3) died of a fe - ver,* And noth - ing could save her, And

(1) there I first met with sweet Mol - ly Ma - lone. She
(2) so were her moth - er and fa - ther be - fore. They
(3) that was the end of sweet Mol - ly Ma - lone. Her

pronounced "fay-ver"

Tzena, Tzena, Tzena

**Words by
Mitchell Parish;
Music by
Issachar Miron
(Michrovsky)
and Julius Grossman**

Who can forget The Weavers (Lee Hays, Fred Hellerman, Ronnie Gilbert and Pete Seeger), the great group of the 1950s who brought us "Goodnight, Irene," "On Top of Old Smoky," "Kisses Sweeter Than Wine" and countless other irresistible songs in the folk-song tradition? One of their most exciting numbers and their first million-selling disc was a version of "Tzena, Tzena, Tzena," which they recorded with Gordon Jenkins and His Orchestra in 1950. "Tzena" was originally written in Hebrew in 1941. Some years later, Mitchell Parish supplied the English lyrics we feature here. Who can possibly resist this lively Israeli dance song? Surely not you. Start dancing!

Tze - na, Tze - na, Tze - na, Tze - na, How can an - y - thing be plain - er
Tze - na, Tze - na, Tze - na, Tze - na, Don't you know your eyes con - tain a

than____ My love for you?____
look____ That thrills me through?____

Words by
A. B. Paterson

Music by
Marie Cowan

"Waltzing Matilda" was sung as a marching song by Australian troops during World War II. American GIs picked it up and brought its catchy tune back home. Using Australian slang, the song tells the story of a drifter (swagman) who camps beside a small

pond (billabong) under the shade of a eucalyptus (coolibah) tree. He steals a sheep (jumbuck) from a squatter (rancher) and escapes the troopers by jumping into the billabong. "Matilda" is a blanket roll in which the swagman carries his possessions.

1. Once a jol-ly swag-man__ Camped__ by a bil-la-bong,
2. Down__ came a jum-buck To drink__ at the bil-la-bong;
3. Up__ rode the squat-ter__ Mount-ed__ on his thor-ough-bred;
4. Up__ jumped the swag-man,__ Sprang in-to the bil-la-bong;

(1) Un-der the shade of a coo-li-bah__ tree, And he sang__ as he watched And__
(2) Up jumped the swag-man and grabbed__him with glee. And he sang__ as he shoved That__
(3) Down came the troop-ers,__ one,__ two,__three.__ "Whose that jol-ly jum-buck__
(4) "You'll nev-er catch me a-live,"__ said__ he. And his ghost__may be heard As you

Twinkle, Twinkle, Little Star

The tune of "Twinkle, Twinkle, Little Star" is probably known just about everywhere in the world. Its strains show up in the work of countless composers. Mozart used it as the basis for a set of piano variations, and Hungarian composer Erno Dohnanyi also used it in *Variations on a Nursery Song*. Although rockets in space are an everyday occurrence, is there anyone who has ever looked at the summer sky all aglow with "twinkling" stars and not wondered about them?

Parody

Starkle, starkle, little twink,
How I wonder what you think!
Up above the world so high,
Think you own the whole darn sky?
Starkle, starkle, little twink,
You're not so great,
That's what I think!

Comin' Thru the Rye

There have been many versions of this Scottish song, including one by the 18th-century poet Robert Burns that was definitely not for children. The one we sing today is set to an old British dance tune called "The Miller's Wedding." Try clapping the rhythm of the melody as you sing.

Stately

If a bod-y meet a bod-y Com-in' through the rye.
If a bod-y meet a bod-y Com-in' frae the town.

If a bod-y kiss a bod-y, Need a bod-y cry.
If a bod-y greet a bod-y, Need a bod-y frown.

Ev-'ry las-sie has her lad-die; Nane, they say, ha'e I. Yet

a' the lads they smile on me When com-in' through the rye.

The Hokey-Pokey

This is a traditional children's dance, in which the instructions in the song are followed. Children usually make a circle, although the movements can be done in almost any formation. The motion for "do the Hokey-Pokey" is a hula-type hip swing with index fingers pointed upward in the air. No motion is necessary for "That's what it's all about," and a clap is given on "Hey." Or, you can clap throughout the last line.

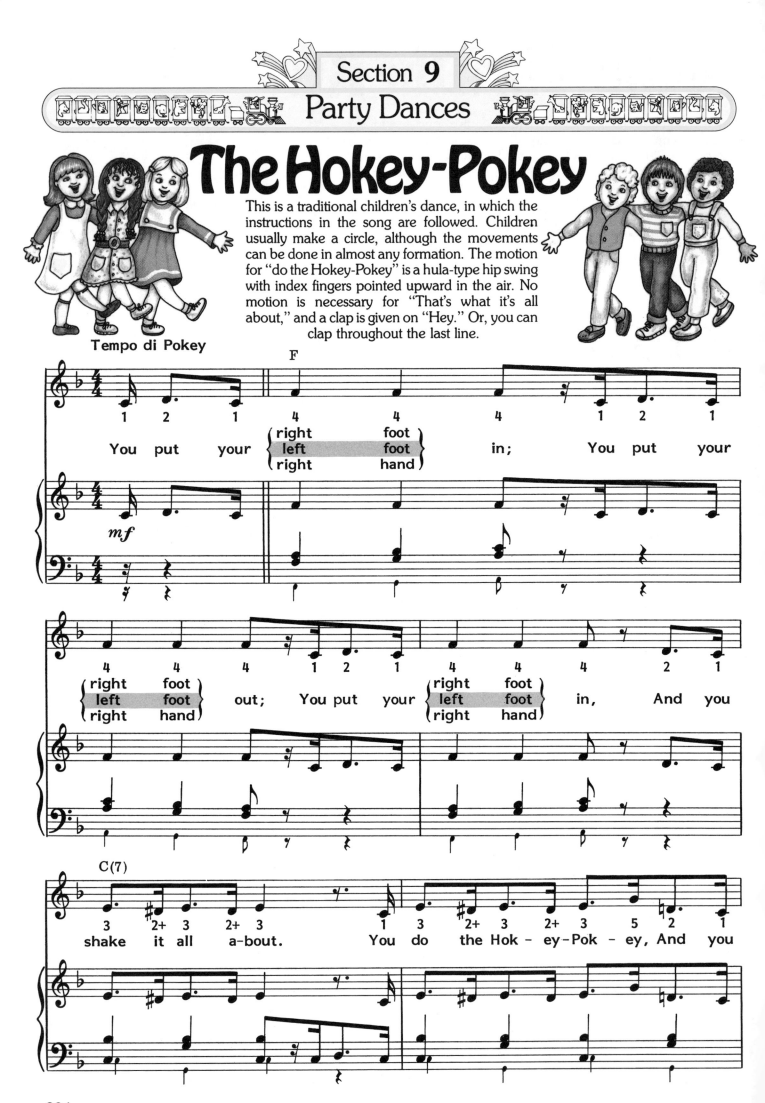

Tempo di Pokey

You put your { right foot / left foot / right hand } in; You put your right foot / left foot / right hand } out; You put your { right foot / left foot / right hand } in, And you shake it all a-bout. You do the Hok-ey-Pok-ey, And you

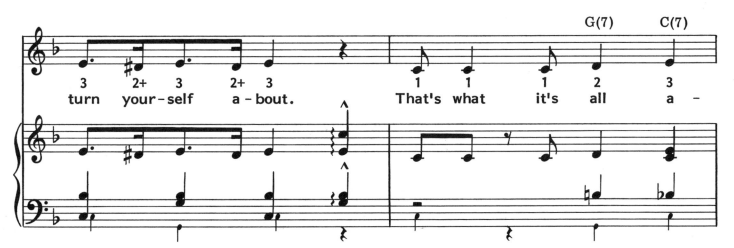

turn your-self a-bout. That's what it's all a-

G(7)   C(7)

For additional words

F

bout.   Hey,   you put   your

Last time

F

bout.   Hey!

(both hands) 8va higher

4. Hey, you put your left hand in;
   You put your left hand out;
   You put your left hand in,
   And you shake it all about.
   You do the Hokey-Pokey,
   And you turn yourself about.
   That's what it's all about.

5. Hey, you put your right shoulder in;
   You put your right shoulder out;
   Etc.

6. Hey, you put your left shoulder in;
   You put your left shoulder out;
   Etc.

7. Hey, you put your right hip in;
   You put your right hip out;
   Etc.

8. Hey, you put your left hip in;
   You put your left hip out;
   Etc.

9. Hey, you put your whole self in;
   You put your whole self out;
   Etc.

Words by Jack Harlen

Music by Frank Bjorn

Written by Bent Fabricius Bjerre under the name Frank Bjorn, "The Alley Cat Song" is danced in a line formation. The tune is played faster and faster, with the dancers becoming more and more frantic as they try to do all the steps. Here's how it's done:

Right foot out to side and then back to touch left foot (two times). Right knee bent and lifted to left, then foot back to floor. Same motion with left knee. Jump one-quarter turn on word "cat" and clap. The whole sequence is then repeated facing in a new direction.

Starting moderately slow; each chorus faster than the previous one

He goes on the prowl each night   Like an al-ley cat,

Look-in' for some new de-light   Like an al-ley cat.

She can't trust him
He don't know what

out of sight,   There's no doubt of that.
faith - ful means,   There's no doubt of that.

He just don't know
He's too bus - y

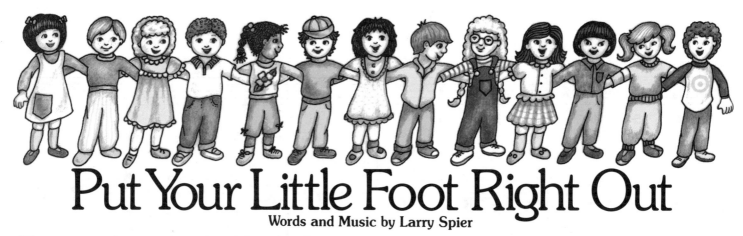

Put Your Little Foot Right Out

Words and Music by Larry Spier

This was a popular party dance for adults in the 1940s and has now become a children's favorite. It began as a folk dance called the varsoviana, which might have originated in Poland and been named for the city of Warsaw. Polish immigrants introduced it in North America, and the dance became well known in rural areas. Then, in 1939, Larry Spier wrote this popularization, and the varsoviana turned into "Put Your Little Foot Right Out."

Put Your Little Foot Right Out

The Bunny Hop

How to do "The Bunny Hop": One beat each — right foot out to side and then back to touch left foot (twice). Left foot to side and back to touch right foot (twice). Two beats each — hop forward, hop backward. Hop forward three times on "Hop, hop, hop!"

Bright blues tempo

Words and Music by Ray Anthony and Leonard Auletti

Put your right foot for-ward; Put your left foot out. Do the Bun-ny Hop.

Hop, hop, hop! Dance this new cre-a-tion; It's the new sen-sa-tion.

Do the Bun-ny Hop. Hop, hop, hop! Let's all join in the fun,—

Fa-ther, moth-er, son. Do the Bun-ny Hop. Hop, hop, hop!

If the tune of this very simple song for learning the letters of the alphabet sounds a bit familiar to you, well, it should. The ubiquitous "Twinkle, Twinkle, Little Star"

The Alphabet Song

shines through once again in this old, traditional children's song. In singing it, try not to make one word out of the letters "L-M-N-O-P." It's a real challenge.

Allegretto, in 2 (♩=1 beat)

F		B♭	F	C(7)	F	C	F

4 4 8 8 9 9 8 6+ 6+ 6 6 5 5 5 5 4
A B C D E F G H I J K L M N O P

mp

C(7)	F	C	F	C(7)	F	C

8 8 6+ 6+ 6 6 5 8 8 6+ 6+ 6 6 5
Q R S and T U V W *(dou-ble - U)* and X Y Z.

F		B♭	F	C(7)	F	Gm(7) C(7) F

4 4 8 8 9 9 8 6+ 6+ 6 6 5 5 4
Now you've heard my A B C; Tell me what you think of me.

slower

212

Remember Your Name and Address

Words by Irving Caesar; Music by Gerald Marks

Irving Caesar's lyrics for "Tea for Two" and "Swanee" are among his best-known works . . . followed closely by his *Songs of Safety* for children, for which Gerald Marks composed the music. With *Songs of Safety*, children sing about not skating on thin ice, not chasing balls that roll into the street and watching out for cars while bicycle-riding. Here, the advice is to "remember your name and address and telephone number too." Pretty good advice!

Moderately flowing

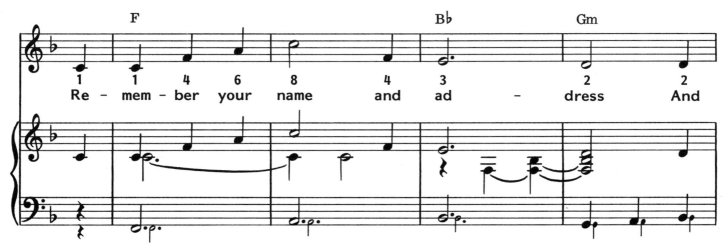

Re - mem - ber your name and ad - dress And

tel - e - phone num - ber too._____ Then

Remember Your Name and Address

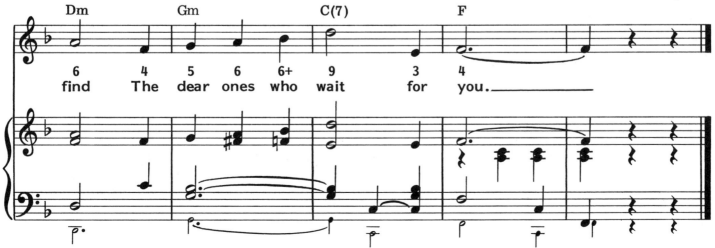

215

The Mulberry Bush

On the first verse of this song, children join hands and move in a circle while singing. On the other verses, they act out the words, in time to the music, while standing in place.

1. Here we go round the mul-ber-ry bush, The mul-ber-ry bush, the
2. This is the way we wash our clothes, We wash our clothes, we
3. This is the way we i-ron our clothes, We i-ron our clothes, we

(1) mul-ber-ry bush. Here we go round the mul-ber-ry bush So
(2) wash our clothes. This is the way we wash our clothes So
(3) i-ron our clothes. This is the way we i-ron our clothes So

For additional words

Final ending

(1) ear-ly in the morn - ing.　　morn - ing.
(2) ear-ly Mon - day morn - ing.
(3) ear-ly Tues - day morn - ing.

4. This is the way we scrub the floor, *etc.*
   So early Wednesday morning.

5. This is the way we mend our clothes, *etc.*
   So early Thursday morning.

6. This is the way we sweep the house, *etc.*
   So early Friday morning.

7. This is the way we bake our bread, *etc.*
   So early Saturday morning.

8. This is the way we go to church, *etc.*
   So early Sunday morning.

216

"Ten Little Indians" is essentially a children's counting song. It was written in the 1860s by Septimus Winner, who also wrote "Oh Where, Oh Where Has My Little Dog Gone?" (see page 86). Children can use the fingers of both hands to keep track of the Indian boys as they sing.

TEN LITTLE INDIANS

Spirited

One lit – tle, two lit – tle, three lit – tle In – dians,
Ten lit – tle, nine lit – tle, eight lit – tle In – dians,

Four lit – tle, five lit – tle, six lit – tle In – dians, Seven lit – tle, eight lit – tle,
Seven lit – tle, six lit – tle, five lit – tle In – dians, Four lit – tle, three lit – tle,

nine lit – tle In – dians, Ten lit – tle In – dian boys.
two lit – tle In – dians, One lit – tle In – dian boy.

217

This Old Man

This traditional English children's game and counting song became popular here after it was used in the 1958 film *The Inn of the Sixth Happiness*. Children can act out the words as they sing, indicating the number they're up to by holding up the appropriate number of fingers.

Brightly, with spirit

1. This old man, he played one; He played knick-knack on my thumb.
2. This old man, he played two; He played knick-knack on my shoe.
3. This old man, he played three; He played knick-knack on my knee.

With a knick-knack, pad-dy whack, Give a dog a bone; This old man came roll-ing home.

4. This old man, he played four;
   He played knick-knack on my door.
   Chorus

5. This old man, he played five;
   He played knick-knack on my hive.
   Chorus

6. This old man, he played six;
   He played knick-knack on my sticks.
   Chorus

7. This old man, he played seven;
   He played knick-knack up in heaven.
   Chorus

8. This old man, he played eight;
   He played knick-knack on my gate.
   Chorus

9. This old man, he played nine;
   He played knick-knack on my spine.
   Chorus

10. This old man, he played ten;
    He played knick-knack once again.
    Chorus

218

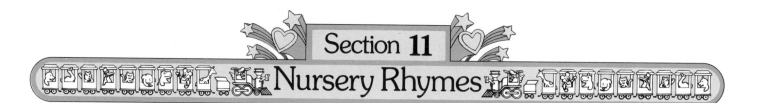

Billy Boy *(page 220)* "Billy Boy" is probably a version of the well-known English ballad "Lord Randal," although the words of that song are much more dramatic than these. It's fun to sing "Billy Boy" as if it were a conversation. One child sings the questions and another, as Billy, the answers.

Little Bo-Peep *(page 221)* This is one of the most popular nursery rhymes of all, one of the group known as *Mother Goose Rhymes*. Like so many other rhymes, it originated in England and certainly dates from the 19th century, if it is not older than that. There was once a child's game called Bo-Peep. Could it be that the sheep in the rhyme are playing Bo-Peep or peek-a-boo with their owner?

Rock-a-Bye Baby *(page 221)* This lullaby originally began "Hush-a-bye baby." But then, in 1872, Effie Crockett, a relative of the famous Davy Crockett, wrote the music that we sing today and changed the opening words. She was 15 at the time and was inspired while baby-sitting for a restless child.

Sing a Song of Sixpence *(page 222)* "Sing a Song of Sixpence" is a nursery rhyme rich in symbolism. Some say the king is Henry VIII; the queen, Henry's first wife, Catherine of Aragon; and the maid, Henry's second wife, Anne Boleyn (who lost her entire head, not just her nose). In any case, the song could be based on fact. There is at least one ancient cookbook that contains a recipe for a pie in which live birds are enclosed and fly out when the pie is cut. Wouldn't you prefer apples or blueberries to birds?

Baa, Baa, Black Sheep *(page 223)* It has been suggested that the words of this very old rhyme point up the class differences between the little boy and the master, probably the King of England. Did you notice that the tune is like that of another song? It's "Twinkle, Twinkle, Little Star" once again!

Jack and Jill *(page 223)* Although from the 15th century on the terms "Jack" and "Jill" came to mean "lad" and "lass," it is possible that the two characters in the original version of this song were both boys. A number of religious connotations and a great deal of intrigue have been read into the words, with the climb to the top of a hill for water having special significance, the water in this case being holy water. Children are more inclined to take the words of the song literally and delight in acting them out.

Hot Cross Buns *(page 224)* This is an old English street cry heard on Good Friday, when some people eat hot cross buns for breakfast. Try playing the first two lines of this song on the piano or another instrument. There are only three different notes in this part. A grownup can show children where to start.

Humpty Dumpty *(page 225)* Some scholars think this rhyme is hundreds and hundreds of years old. Whatever its age, it is known in some version by most children in the Western Hemisphere. It's so familiar that people don't realize it's a riddle. For what is this Humpty Dumpty that cannot be put together again? It's an egg, of course.

Little Jack Horner *(page 225)* There probably was a real Jack Horner. He lived in England at the time of Henry VIII, and was a steward to a wealthy abbot. The story has it that his employer sent Jack to the King with a gift "pie" containing the deeds to several large estates. Jack put in his thumb, pulled out a deed . . . and lived happily ever after on one of the estates.

Hey, Diddle, Diddle *(page 226)* Although many "hidden" meanings have been found in the words of this rhyme (the cat supposedly represents Queen Elizabeth I), the only certain thing to be said about "Hey, Diddle, Diddle" is that it first appeared in print in an English publication of the late 18th century called *Mother Goose's Melody*. The words are probably just nonsense that are fun to sing and act out.

Little Boy Blue *(page 226)* There is some disagreement about the identity of Little Boy Blue. One theory is that he was meant to be Cardinal Wolsey of England, who was the son of a butcher and probably did look after sheep as a child. Whoever Boy Blue was, he obviously forsook his duties. The moral of this rhyme is: Pay attention to the job at hand!

Little Miss Muffet *(page 227)* This is a very popular nursery rhyme . . . and a very scary one too. Do you know what the words mean? "Curds and whey" are the solid and watery parts of milk when it separates. And, according to the dictionary, a "tuffet" is a low seat or stool. Most important, it rhymes with Muffet. Who's afraid of a cute little spider anyway?

There Was an Old Woman Who Lived in a Shoe *(page 227)* Many nursery rhymes started as political satires. In this one, for example, the "old woman" might have been the British Parliament and her "children," the many colonies under British rule. Taken literally, a shoe seems an unlikely place to house so many children, and artists through the ages have had fun portraying this silly home. Child artists might also enjoy trying to draw a picture of it.

Oats, Peas, Beans and Barley Grow *(page 228)* The complete version of this song has led to the belief that it originally may have had a religious and symbolic meaning and been part of farmers' spring rites to promote the fertility of their fields.

Lazy Mary, Will You Get Up? *(page 228)* This traditional children's song is sometimes played as a game in which the child who is playing the mother tempts the child who is Mary to get up. She offers such things as "a slice of bread and a cup of tea," which draw a negative response. Then she might offer "a nice young man with rosy cheeks," which elicits a positive "Yes, Mother, I will get up." Today, Mary is already up—and at work. She's an executive of a corporation.

Old King Cole *(page 229)* Although there were three English kings with this name, the one in this song is reported to be that King Cole who reigned in Britain in the 3rd century. He was obviously not only merry but a music lover as well. And that's surely a fine recommendation.

Little Bo-Peep

Slowly

C			F	G			C	
5	8	3	7	6	5	2	3	2
Lit – tle		Bo – Peep	has	lost	her	sheep	And	

Am	C/G		Em	C	F		C	
1	1	1 2	3	5	3	6 6 6	5	5
can't	tell	where_ to	find	them.		Leave them a – lone	and	

G(7)			F	C		G(7)		C
4	3	2	8 7 6	5 3	1	2		1
they'll	come	home,	Wag-ging their	tails_	be – hind			them.

Rock-a-Bye Baby

Allegretto

Bb				F(7)	
2 4	9	8	6+	2 4 6+	6
Rock – a-bye, ba – by,) Hush – a-bye, ba – by,)				On the tree - top.	

		Bb			
2+ 4	9+ 9	8	8 6+ 5	4	2 4 9 8 6+
When the wind blows,		The	cra-dle will	rock.	When the bough breaks, The

F(7)	Bb	Eb	Bb	Cm	F(7)	Bb
2 4 6+	6 5	4 6+ 9+	9 6+	8 5	6	6+
cra – dle will fall,	And	down will come	ba – by,	Cra-dle	and	all.

Sing a Song of Sixpence

Moderately

Sing a song of six - pence, A pock - et full of rye;

Four and twen-ty black-birds Baked in a pie. When the pie was o-pened, The

birds be-gan to sing. Was-n't that a dain-ty dish To set be-fore the king? The

king was in the count-ing-house, Count-ing out his mon-ey. The

queen was in the par-lor, Eat-ing bread and hon-ey. The maid was in the gar-den,

Hang-ing out the clothes; A - long_ came a black-bird And pecked_ off her nose.

Both arrangements: Copyright © 1985 Ardee Music Publishing, Inc.

Humpty Dumpty

Moderately

D   A(7)

6   9   4+   6   2   3   4+   3   5   7   3   5

Hump - ty Dump - ty sat on a wall; Hump - ty Dump - ty

A(7)   D   G   D   G

1+   4+   3   2   4+   5   6   7   6   5   4+   5   6   7

had a great fall. All the king's hors - es and all the king's men

D   A   D   Em   D   A(7)   D

2   2   2   3   3   4+   5   5   6   3   4+   2

Could - n't put Hump - ty Dump - ty to - geth - er a - gain.____

Little Jack Horner

Moderately

F   A(7)   B♭   G(7)

1   1   1   4   3   2   2   2   5   4

Lit - tle Jack Hor - ner Sat in a cor - ner,

C(7)   F   A(7)

3   3   3   6   5   4   1   1   1   1   4   3

Eat - ing his Christ - mas pie.____ He stuck in his thumb And

B♭   G(7)   C(7)   F

2   2   2   5   4   3   9   8   6+   2   3   4

pulled out a plum, And said, "What a good boy am I."____

HEY, DIDDLE, DIDDLE

Moderately

F / C(7)

6	6	6	6	6+	8	5	5	5	5	4	5
Hey,	did	– dle,	did	– dle,	The	cat	and	the	fid	– dle,	The

F / C(7) / Bb

6	6	6	6+	8	5	6	6+	6+	6+	6+	8	9
cow	jumped	o	– ver	the	moon.		The	lit	– tle	dog	laughed	To

F / Dm / F / C(7) / F

8	6	4	5	6	1	1	1	1	2	3	4
see	such	sport,	And	the	dish	ran	a	– way	with	the	spoon.

Little Boy Blue

Moderately

F / C(7) / F / C(7)

1	4	2	3	2	1	4	2	3	2
Lit	– tle	Boy	Blue,		come	blow	on	your	horn;	There's

F / G(7) / C(7) / F / Bb

1	4	5	6	5	4	6	5	4	8	8	6	4	2	2	2
sheep	in	the	mead	– ow	and	cows	in	the	corn.	Where	is	the	boy	who	looks

C(7) / F / Bb / Gm / F / C(7) / F

6+	5	3	1	4	2	3	4	8	6+	6	5	4
af	– ter	the	sheep?	He	lies	in	the	hay	– stack,	fast	a	– sleep.

226

Little Miss Muffet

Allegretto

Lit - tle Miss Muf - fet Sat on a tuf - fet,
Eat - ing some curds and whey.___ There came a big spi - der And
sat down be - side her, And fright - ened Miss Muf - fet a - way.___

There Was an Old Woman Who Lived in a Shoe

Moderately, in 1 (♩.=1 beat)

There_ was an old wom - an who lived in a shoe; She had
so man - y chil - dren, she did-n't know what to do. She_
gave them some broth with - out an - y bread; She_
whipped them all sound - ly and put them to bed.

Oats, Peas, Beans and Barley Grow

Brightly (♩.=1 beat)

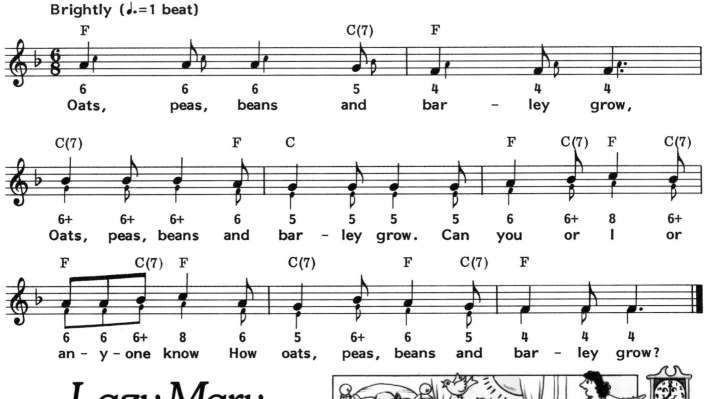

F				C(7)	F	

6   6   6   5   4   4   4

Oats,   peas,   beans   and   bar - ley   grow,

C(7)   F   C   F   C(7)   F   C(7)

6+   6+   6+   6   5   5   5   5   6   6+   8   6+

Oats, peas, beans and bar - ley grow. Can you or I or

F   C(7)   F   C(7)   F   C(7)   F

6   6   6+   8   6   5   6+   6   5   4   4   4

an - y - one know How oats, peas, beans and bar - ley grow?

Lazy Mary, Will You Get Up?

With spirit

F

4   4   4   4   6   8   6   4   4   5   6   5   6

La - zy Mar - y, will you get up, Will you get up, Will
Oh, no, Moth - er, I won't get up, I won't get up, I

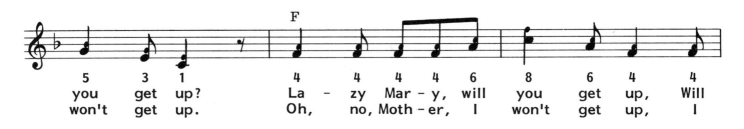

		F				

5   3   1   4   4   4   4   6   8   6   4   4

you get up?   La - zy Mar - y, will you get up, Will
won't get up.   Oh, no, Moth - er, I won't get up, I

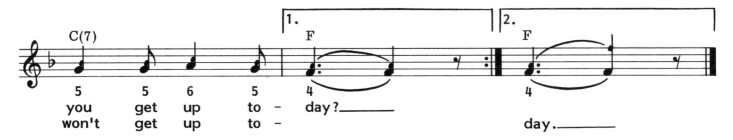

C(7)   **1.** F   **2.** F

5   5   6   5   4   4

you get up to - day?_____
won't get up to -   day._____

228

229

London Bridge (*page 230*) On the first verse of this extremely old game song, two children stand opposite one another while the other participants walk between them, around behind them and between them again. On the second verse, the two children who represent the bridge join one hand, making half an arch for the others to walk through. On the next verse, they join both hands. Finally, they drop both joined hands, "trapping" whichever child is between them at the moment. Rocking the child back and forth, they sing, "Take the key and lock her (him) up." Although London Bridge has become famous for falling down, it actually stood sturdily over the Thames River in London for 600 years. Then, in 1826, a new London Bridge was built to replace it. That bridge has since been replaced also, and in 1968 it was moved to the United States. Today it stands not in London but in Arizona.

Eensy, Weensy Spider (*page 231*) Children enjoy singing this song with a finger-play. By touching opposite index fingers and thumbs, children can pretend to walk the "Eensy, Weensy Spider" up a waterspout. The illustrations with the song on the following page show the rest of the actions.

London Bridge

Allegretto

	8	9	8	6+	6	6+	8
1.	Lon	don	Bridge	is	fall	ing	down,
2.	Build	it	up	with	i	ron	bars,
3.	Build	it	up	with	gold	and	silver,
4.	Take	the	key	and	lock	her	up,

	5	6	6+	6	6+	8	8	9	8	6+
(1)	fall	ing	down,	fall	ing	down.	Lon	don	Bridge	is
(2)	i	ron	bars,	i	ron	bars.	Build	it	up	with
(3)	gold	and	silver,	gold	and	silver.	Build	it	up	with
(4)	lock	her	up,	lock	her	up.	Take	the	key	and

	6	6+	8	5	8	6	4
(1)	fall	ing	down,	My	fair	la	dy.
(2)	i	ron	bars,	My	fair	la	dy.
(3)	gold	and	silver,	My	fair	la	dy.
(4)	lock	her	up,	My	fair	la	dy.

The Farmer in the Dell *(page 232)* To play this game song, a group of children pick a boy or girl to be the farmer and form a circle around him or her. They sing as they circle around, then stop while the farmer selects someone to be his wife. The wife joins him in the center of the circle, and the selection process continues until the rat takes the cheese. Then all of the children can run away except the cheese, or the children can begin a new set of verses, starting with "The farmer runs away" (back to the outer circle) until only the cheese is left. The cheese can be the farmer in the next game. It takes quite a few participants to play "The Farmer in the Dell." Try it at your next birthday party, or just sing it for fun with a group of your friends.

Hickory, Dickory, Dock *(page 232)* The clock in question in this rhyme was probably a large grandfather's clock and when it chimed it must have scared the poor little mouse. Pretend your fingers are the mouse running up the clock. Then see how fast you can get them to run down when the clock strikes one o'clock. "Hickory, Dickory, Dock" is one of the group of rhymes that were usually published together and called *Mother Goose Rhymes*.

The Farmer in the Dell

Moderately

F

| 1 | 4 | 4 | 4 | 4 | 4 | | 5 | 6 | 6 | 6 | 6 | 6 |

The farm – er in the dell, The farm – er in the dell,

C(7)   F

| 8 | 8 | 9 | 8 | 6 | 4 | 5 | 6 | 6 | 5 | 5 | 4 |

Heigh – ho, the der – ry – o, The farm – er in the dell.

2. The farmer takes a wife, *etc.*
3. The wife takes the child, *etc.*
4. The child takes the nurse, *etc.*
5. The nurse takes the dog, *etc.*

6. The dog takes the cat, *etc.*
7. The cat takes the rat, *etc.*
8. The rat takes the cheese, *etc.*
9. The cheese stands alone, *etc.*

Hickory, Dickory, Dock

Moderately

F   C(7)   F   C(7)

| 6 | 6+ | 8 | 6+ | 6 | 5 | 6 | | 6 |

Hick – o – ry, dick – o – ry, dock, The

F   C(7)   F   C(7)   F

| 6 | 8 | 6+ | 5 | 6 | 6 | 6 | 6 | 8 | 8 |

mouse ran up the clock. The clock struck one; The

Bb   F   C(7)   F

| 6+ | 6+ | 9 | 8 | 9 | 8 | 6+ | 6 | 5 | 4 | 8 9 10 11 |

mouse ran down, Hick-o-ry, dick-o-ry, dock.

232

Section 13
Songs That Go Round and Round

ALL ABOUT ROUNDS

Rounds are songs that are specially created so that various parts of the song can be sung simultaneously by different individuals or groups with musically pleasant results.

It is best to learn the song very well before trying to sing it as a round.

A round can be sung in as many parts as the music indicates, but any round can be sung in just two parts if desired. In the three rounds in this section (**"Three Blind Mice," "Row, Row, Row Your Boat"** and **"Frère Jacques"**), only two people are needed, but the more singers you have on each part, the easier it is to perform.

Decide how many times the round will be sung through and assign the singers to each part. Each group starts from the beginning of the song at the point in the music where the group's number is indicated.

If your friends are experienced singers, it is possible for everyone to start and end a round at the same time. This is done by having one group start at the beginning while the others start precisely where their numbers are in the music. Each group continues singing to the end and goes back to the beginning as many times as desired. Then, on signal, everyone holds the last note of the phrase and stops singing at once. The effect is quite dramatic.

Three Blind Mice

Moderately

Three blind mice!___ Three blind mice!___ See how they run!___ See how they run!___ They all ran af-ter the farm-er's wife, Who cut off their tails with a carv-ing knife. Did you ev-er see such a sight in your life As three blind mice?___

Row, Row, Row Your Boat

With energy

1 C ... **2** ...

1   1   1   2   3   3   2 3   4   5

Row,   row,   row your boat   Gent - ly down the stream,

3 ... G(7) ... C

8 8 8   5 5 5   3 3 3   1 1 1   5   4 3   2 1

Mer-ri-ly, mer-ri-ly, mer-ri-ly, mer-ri-ly, Life is but a dream.

FRÈRE JACQUES

Moderately

1 F C(7) F   F C(7) F   **2** F C(7) F

4   5   6   4   4   5   6   4   6   6+   8

*Frè - re Jac - ques, Frè - re Jac - ques, dor - mez vous,

Are you sleep - ing, Are you sleep - ing, Broth - er John,

F C(7) F   **3** F C(7) F   F C(7) F

6   6+   8   8   9   8 6+ 6   4   8   9   8 6+ 6   4

Dor - mez vous?   Son - nez les ma - tin - es, Son-nez les ma - tin - es,

Broth - er John?   Morn - ing bells are ring - ing, Morn-ing bells are ring - ing,

4 F C(7) F   **1.** F C(7) F   **2.** F C(7) F

4   1   4   4   1   4   4   1   4

Din din don,   Din din don.   Din din don.

Ding dong ding,   Ding dong ding.   Ding dong ding.

For pronunciation of French words, see page 36 of the lyric booklet.

Rudolph the Red-Nosed Reindeer

Words and Music by Johnny Marks

In 1939, a copywriter for Montgomery Ward created Rudolph for an advertising pamphlet. Ten years later, Johnny Marks immortalized Rudy in song (a best-selling recording for Gene Autry). Next to "White Christmas," "Rudolph" has sold more copies than any other contemporary song.

Rudolph the Red-Nosed Reindeer

Santa Claus is comin' to town

Words and Music by J. Fred Coots and Haven Gillespie

Comedian Eddie Cantor introduced this song on his radio show in 1934, and it became an instant hit. Interestingly, the composers couldn't find a publisher when they wrote it two years earlier, because everyone thought it was just a "kiddie" song. All children know that they have to be good, especially at Christmastime, if they expect Santa to pay them a visit.

Brightly, with spirit

You bet – ter watch out; you bet – ter not cry;
mak – ing a list and check – ing it twice;

Bet – ter not pout; I'm tell – ing you why: San – ta Claus is com – in' to
Gon – na find out who's naugh – ty and nice: San – ta Claus is com – in' to

1.
town. He's

2.
town. He

FROSTY THE SNOW MAN

Gene Autry recorded "Frosty" in 1951, and that cute little snowman did more than "dance around." He took right off and sold more than a million discs for Columbia Records. It's easy to imagine a snowman coming to life, and fortunately for all of us, Frosty does just that every holiday season.

Words and Music by Steve Nelson and Jack Rollins

Moderately, in 2 (♩=1 beat)

Fros - ty the Snow Man was a jol - ly, hap - py soul, With a
Fros - ty the Snow Man knew the sun was hot that day, So he

corn - cob pipe and a but - ton nose and two eyes made out of coal.
said, "Let's run and we'll have some fun now be - fore I melt a - way."

240

Frosty the Snow Man

Peter Cottontail

Words and Music by Steve Nelson and Jack Rollins

The same folks who brought you "Frosty the Snow Man" created "Peter Cottontail," who, thanks to Gene Autry's recording, hopped into our lives in 1951 with great success. Ever since Beatrix Potter wrote *The Tale of Peter Rabbit*, Peter seems to be the fitting name for a bunny. If you see one "hippity hoppin'" on Easter Day, try calling it "Peter." If you get no response, try a girl's name instead.

Here comes Pe - ter Cot - ton - tail,
Hop - pin' down the bun - ny trail,

Hip - pi - ty hop - pin', Eas - ter's on its way.
Look at him stop and lis - ten to him say:

Peter Cottontail

Year-Round Version

Look at Peter Cottontail,
Hoppin' down the bunny trail,
A rabbit of distinction, so they say.
He's the king of Bunnyland
'Cause his eyes are shiny, and
He can spot the wolf a mile away.
When the others go for clover
And the big bad wolf appears,
He's the one that's watching over,
Givin' signals with his ears.
And that's why folks in Rabbit Town
Feel so free when he's aroun';
Peter's helpin' someone ev'ry day.

Little Peter Cottontail,
Hoppin' down the bunny trail,
Happened to stop for carrots on the way.
Something told him it was wrong;
Farmer Jones might come along,
And an awful price he'd have to pay.
But he knew his legs were faster,
So he nibbled three or four,
And he almost met disaster
When he heard that shotgun roar.
Oh, that's how Peter Cottontail,
Hoppin' down the bunny trail,
Lost his tail but still he got away.

Honor Your Parents

**Words and Music by
Glenn Wilkinson and Mary Gross**

"Honor Your Parents," one of the songs included in *Sir Oliver's Song*, a record album that was intended to teach children the Ten Commandments, was written by Glenn Wilkinson and Mary Gross. There's a sound old-fashioned message in this song that children and adults alike should heed. Respect your parents — they do so much for you.

Happily (♩. = 1 beat)

mf

F

8 4 4 5 6 5 4 2 2 2 2 1 4 4 5 6 5 4

Bb/F

F

1. I nev-er have seen me a hap-pi-er lass Than one al-ways do-in' the
(2) nev-er have seen me a hap-pi-er lad Than one who's o-bey-ing his
(3) thank-ful for all that your mum and dad do, And do all you can to make

G(7)   **C(7)**   **F**   **Bb/F**

5 5 6 5 1 4 4 5 6 5 4 2 2 2 2 4 6

(1) things that she's asked. She joy-ful-ly does what her mum and dad say, And she
(2) moth-er and dad. He does-n't talk back when he's told what to do, But he
(3) them proud of you. And if you be look-ing for your pot of gold, You'll be

The Niña, the Pinta, the Santa María

Words and Music by Ruth Roberts and Bill Katz

"The Niña, the Pinta and the Santa María" is a perfect song to sing on Columbus Day, which celebrates the discovery of America by Christopher Columbus in 1492. The Italian navigator sailed from Spain in three small ships — named, as we all know, the *Niña*, the *Pinta* and the *Santa María*.

Moderately bright waltz

1. There were

(1) three lit - tle ships in the har - bor,_____ As lone - ly as
(2) long came a man named Co - lum - bus,_____ Who said that the
(3) filled them with food and with wa - ter_____ And sail - ors to

(1) they could be,_____ 'Cause no - bod - y want - ed to
(2) world was round._____ He plead - ed with Queen Is - a -
(3) steer each ship._____ The big - ger boats laughed in the

248

* (pronounced "Neen-ya")

4. (The) ocean was windy and stormy;
The waves were as high as could be.
The load was so heavy to carry,
But on went the brave little three.
The *Niña*, the *Pinta*, the *Santa María*,
On went the brave little three.

5. At last came the day when Columbus
Sighted America's shore.
Just think he might never have found it
If it hadn't been for
The *Niña*, the *Pinta*, the *Santa María*
Sailed to America's shore.

YANKEE DOODLE

There are many conjectures about the origin of "Yankee Doodle." What seems closest to the truth is that the tune is that of an Irish jig and the words are English. The British sang it during the American Revolution to make fun of the Continental Army, but the colonists loved the song and later took it as their own.

With spirit

1. Yan - kee Doo - dle went to town A - rid - ing on a po - ny,
2. Fath'r and I went down to camp A - long with Cap - tain Good - in.
3. There was Cap - tain Wash - ing - ton Up - on a slap - ping stal - lion,

(1) Stuck a feath - er in his cap And called it mac - a - ro - ni.
(2) There we saw the men and boys As thick as has - ty pud - din'.
(3) Giv - ing or - ders to his men; I guess there were a mil - lion.

Yan - kee Doo - dle keep it up, Yan - kee Doo - dle dan - dy.

Mind the mu - sic and the step And with the girls be han - dy.

250

We Gather Together

This beautiful old hymn is often sung to celebrate Thanksgiving Day, a day set aside for feasting and prayers to give thanks to God for the year's blessings. In the United States, Thanksgiving Day celebrates the Pilgrims' first thanksgiving in 1621 and is observed on the fourth Thursday in November. In Canada, Thanksgiving Day is the second Monday in October.

to Ask the Lord's Blessing

1. We gather together to ask the Lord's blessing; He chastens and hastens His will to make known. The wicked oppressing now cease from distressing; Sing praises to His name; He forgets not His own.

2. Beside us to guide us, our God with us joining, Ordaining, maintaining His kingdom divine. So from the beginning the fight we were winning; Thou, Lord, wast at our side: All glory be Thine!

3. We all do extol Thee, Thou leader triumphant, And pray that Thou still our defender wilt be. Let Thy congregation escape tribulation; Thy name be ever praised! O Lord, make us free!

Can there be anyone who doesn't know this song? But how many people are aware that it was written by two sisters, Mildred and Patty Hill (it was originally called "Good Morning to All"), and that they made a small fortune from its eight measures of music? It's fun to be the birthday person and have your friends sing the song to you . . . and it's also fun to sing it to a dear friend when he or she is celebrating a birthday.

Happy Birthday to You

Words and Music by Mildred Hill and Patty Hill